L L A M A S

An Introduction To Care, Training, and Handling

Most alpine books are available at special quantity discounts for bulk purchases for club promotions, premiums, fund raising, breeder or educational use. Special premium editions or book excerpts can also be created to fit specific needs.

For details, write or telephone Special Markets, Alpine Publications, P.O. Box 7027, Loveland, CO 80537; (303) 667-2017.

L L A M A S

An Introduction To Care, Training, and Handling

SANDI BURT

Alpine Publications Inc.

ISBN 0-931866-49-9

Library of Congress Cataloging-in-Publication Data

Burt, Sandi, 1940–
    Llamas : an introduction to care, training, and handling / Sandi Burt.
        p.   cm.
    Includes index.
    ISBN 0-931866-49-9
    1. Llamas as pets.   I. Title.
SF459.L52B87   1991
636.2'96—dc20

Typography and Interior Design: *Ruth Koning, Shadow Canyon Graphics, Evergreen, Colorado 80439*

Cover Design: *Dianne Borneman, Shadow Canyon Graphics, Evergreen, Colorado 80439*

Front Cover Photo: *Llama and boy at high tide, Camden, Maine. By Jay Stager, Downeast Llamas, Camden, Maine*

Back Cover Photo: *By Doug Sharp, Sharp's Llamas, Petaluma, California*

Printed in the United States of America

―――――――――

To

Tristin, my daughter, who will always have

that special part of my heart;

Toby, my son, my seeker — may he find his quest;

and to all the llamas

CONTENTS

ACKNOWLEDGMENTS

To all of our friends and fellow llama afficiandos who over the years have shared experiences, shows, problems and successes: Paul and Betty Barkman; Fred Bauer, who got us started in llamas; Dick and Virginia Christensen; Bob and Claudia Frost and Michelle Brakebill, who shared their ideas; The Garin Family; Lynn and Judie Hyder, who taught us the art of showmanship; The Jorgensen Family, Triple J Farms; Roberta and Tom Lloyd; Francie Greth-Peto; Sonny and Sue Rodgers; Jim and Susan Rootness, who shared their children; Edie Rosenaur, who allowed me to photograph her beautiful pastures and llamas; Doug and Jamie Sharp, who were always available to answer the night time calls about the critical newborns; and to Joan and Oscar Thompson.

Over the years I have attended several seminars, workshops, and Expos. I would like to thank all the speakers who helped me gain the knowledge to write this book, in particular: William E. Barnett, D.V.M.; Walter Bravo, D.V.M., for his dedicated research in camelids; Murray E. Fowler, D.,V.,M., University of California, Davis, a pioneer in Camelid veterinary care and a friend to all llama lovers; Eric Hoffman; La Rue Johnson, D.V.M., Colorado Statee University, for his tremendous contributions in the fields of nutrition and reproduction; Julie Farver koenig; Daniel Schoenthal and Bradford B. Smith, D.V.M..

My heartfelt thanks go to four very special individuals: Betty McKinney, Editor and Publisher of Alpine Publications, who believed in the need for this book and gave me the chance. Jenné Andrews, editorial assistant, who spent countless hours on rewrites, development and advice. She made me reach a little bit further and encouraged me during my dark hours. Joan Mayerle, my mentor and friend, who listened to my frustrations, lent me her shoulder, and told me to go back to the typewriter. And to Rick Frey, D.V.M., Loomis Basin Veterinary Clinic, who reviewed my technical data, answered thousands of questions, cared for our herd the wee hours of many mornings and became a dear friend. Without these, this book would not have been possible.

FOREWORD

The appearance of a new book on llamas awakens interest and curiosity and gives us the opportunity to share experiences with its author.

Although Sandi Burt's book is geared primarily to the new and prospective llama owner, even long time breeders have only a cursory understanding of all aspects of llama welfare and behavior due to not being able to experience each situation first hand. Therefore, Sandi's incorporating some of her own personal successes and failures may be found invaluable to all of us as we deal with that distinct llama personality on a day to day basis.

Like all books that have included medical sections dealing with numerous illnesses and accidents, it may appear to the reader that the llama is beset on every hand with threats to his well-being. Happily this is not the case, but llamas do become ill and occasionally have accidents, (some early owners believed them to be infallible) and Sandi touches upon some common and not so common problems, we are better able to know when to call upon our verterinarian before a problem becomes irreversible.

Sandi also addresses her fears about the practice of inbreeding in the llama community and the need to be especially cautious in choosing mating partners. It is a known fact that more crias (llama babies) are being born with genetic defects than in any other animal industry today, and Sandi points out that culling in the llama business is relatively nil. Her stressing correct conformation and genetic soundness in any breeding program is indeed a responsible attitude and one that should be applauded.

A chapter on showing is included and contains some excellent information and photos for those owners interested in this facet of llama ownership. There are some good pointers on how to groom, what type of clothing an exhibitor should wear and some ring procedures that one might encounter. Types of classes and definitions are also addressed in this seciton. Though some animal enthusiasts might not agree, llama shows are a definite part of todays industry and the industry of the future. However, we need guidance in this area to insure that the llama's best interest is kept foremost in mind in order to alleviate undue stress and physical exhaustion. Then, and only then, can shows be displayed as a first rate marketing tool. There are organizations today working toward this high quality goal.

It is refreshing, to say the least, that Sandi can "poke fun" at some of her earlier trials and errors. In this manner she aids the newcomer in overcoming his or her's hesitation in asking a "dumb question". We have all been there at one time or another and Sandi is humble enough to share with us that she has been there and back on more than one occasion. This is indeed reassuring for the prospective owner.

I feel you will find this work a valuable collection of information.

VIRGINIA CHRISTENSEN
1990

PREFACE

When you meet a llama, it's almost a mystical experience. You sink into those huge, velvety brown eyes, and a feeling of peace settles over you. When Don and I saw our first llama, llama fever struck! We knew at once that we had to have one . . . or two . . . or three. Our desire became almost an obsession. But where did we begin? Where could we buy them? What did they eat? Did we have enough room? What would we do with them?

We had hundreds of questions, and there were few answers. I visited several libraries and found little information. We gleaned what we could from newspapers and magazine articles. Finally, we visited a llama ranch, and found an owner eager to share information. Soon we began visiting other such ranches, talking with veterinarians and at last, purchased our first two males. Our quest was very much a matter of gathering, incorporating, and experimenting with what we had been told. If I asked ten different breeders one question, I got ten different answers.

We attended workshops, seminars and shows. We subscribed to various organizations, newsletters and magazines. But it was our trial and error experimentaion that taught us the most.

As I wondered why more hasn't been written about llamas, I decided to share our experiences as a kind of llama "primer." I have tried to steer away from the technical and the absolute, and encourage you to consult your own veterinarian about specific problems. Weigh what we share in the light of your own experience. After all, experimentation and growth are all part of the challenge of owning and raising the mystical llama!

CHAPTER ONE

SHIP OF THE ANDES

It is not uncommon to encounter llamas carrying packs on wilderness trails with human companions striding at their sides. Or, out for a Sunday stroll in a rural neighborhood, you may see a pair of these fascinating creatures look up from their browsing and step quietly across a backyard pasture to investigate you. They look intently at you with great, dark eyes, long ears tipped forward. You are captivated, intrigued; what, exactly *is* a llama?

Some say the llama (the double "L" is given the Spanish pronunciation of "Y" in South America) is a cross between a Jack Rabbit, a mule, a camel, a deer and a goat. However, Webster defines him this way:

> Any of several wild and domesticated South American ruminants related to the camels but smaller and without a hump. specif: The domesticated variety of the Guanaco that is about three feet high at the shoulder with a coat of long, coarse wooly hair varying in color from black to white and that has been used for centuries in the Andes as a beast of burden and a source of wool.

The definition in the Holt Intermediate Dictionary reads:

> South American cud-chewing mammal related to the camel but having no hump. It is often used as a beast of burden and its long, light brown or white hair is valued as a fiber for making cloth.

Much conflicting information has been published about the llama. Some sources report the average height to be three feet at the shoulder, others, four. A few writers claim that females should be bred between the ages of two-and-one-half to three years of age. Today many llama ranchers begin breeding them at one year to eighteen months. In

1

short, until recently, information on the llama has been sketchy, even contradictory.

Biological classification of the llama appears below:

Class	*Mammalia*
Order	*Artiodactyla*
Sub-order	*Tylopoda*
Family	*Camelidae*
Genus	*Lama*
Species	*Glama*

ORIGINS

Surprisingly, llamas originated in the western part of North America. Scientists have determined from fossils that the first llamas were about a foot tall, similar to the eohippus or "dawn horse." It is now believed that some of these mini-llamas migrated over a land bridge at the Bering Strait to Asia where they developed into the camel; others migrated south to the Andes, primarily into the areas we now know as Peru and Bolivia, where they evolved into llamas as we know them today.

Three other species of camelids, the alpaca, the guanaco and the vicuna, all native to South America, are the llama's cousins. The alpaca, woollier and smaller than the llama, is domesticated and used mainly for wool production. Its fleece is highly prized the world over. The guanaco is still found in the wild and has distinct coloration. Most of the body is cinnamon-colored with white on inner legs and belly; soft shades of grey intermingle with the cinnamon. Guanacos look like deer, with their tall lanky legs and leanness. Their faces are delicately sculptured and quite beautiful. Vicunas are the least known of the camelids. Since they are highly protected in South America where they are considered endangered, we hear little about them today. Theirs is a soft reddish fiber, the most precious of the camelid wool. More distant cousins are bactrian and dromedary camels. The bactrian has two humps and is found in Central Asia; dromedaries have one hump and inhabit Africa and the Middle East.

EARLY DOMESTICATION

The Incas highly revered llamas and sacrificed them during special religious rites. The Incas believed that llamas had a special relationship

Driving the Llamas to the trailhead for a Peru trek
with Mama's Llamas. *Courtesy of Francie Greth-Peto.*

with the Sun God due to their curious habit of facing the sunrise and
sunset. For centuries, Indians used the llama for carrying their goods
in mining and in transportation. They used only the males for transport; females were kept for breeding. Wool was spun for blankets,
ropes and hats. The strong hides were tanned for sandals and manure
was burned for fuel. Llama meat tastes like lamb and is still today a
part of the South American Indian diet.

Yesterday's llama was truly a utilitarian animal. Their domestication
marked the beginning of a high dependence on them by Andean
culture. Indians measured their wealth by the number of llamas they
possessed. The Spaniards are attributed with naming the llama "Ship
of the Andes" after viewing their remarkable ability to carry goods
over the formidable mountain terrain. According to Stan Ebel in his
introduction on the llama industry in *Llama Medicine,* 1989,:

> The land of the Incas varied from sea level to an elevation of
> more than 15,000 feet. The llama's adaptability and efficiency as
> a pack animal in this varied terrain made it possible to link the
> diverse ecologic zones and to cover the great linear distances of

the Andean region. The llama was bred specifically to produce a large, strong animal for the packing function, while the alpaca was bred to accentuate its naturally finer wool. The harvest of this fine wool served as the base for a significant domestic textile market.

However during the early 1500's, the llamas moved into the sidelines when the Spaniards introduced sheep and other domestics from Europe. Now, llamas are once again in the spotlight as Andean countries recognize their importance as part of the culture and history.

LLAMAS IN NORTH AMERICA

Llamas were introduced into zoos on the eastern seaboard of the United States during the 1870's. However, an import ban in 1930 on all South American hoofed animals because of fears of an outbreak of foot and mouth disease, restricted growth of the North American llama population for many decades.

William Randolph Hearst has been credited as the first breeder to import llamas to the United States in the early 1900's. But his herd at San Simeon, California, was small and unprolific. When he died, the herd numbered between thirty and forty animals.

Richard and Kay Patterson of Sisters, Oregon, have had the greatest impact on the growth of the llama industry in the United States. In 1959, the Pattersons, Arabian horse breeders, began raising guanacos as a hobby. In the early 1970's, they sold the guanaco herd and purchased nine pairs of llamas from the Catskill Game Farm. From 1973 on, Richard and Kay continued to purchase llamas from Catskill and other breeders. The Pattersons also acquired the Jerry Berman herd of 86 llamas from California. In 1979, the Patterson herd became the largest in the United States with over 500 animals. Some of the most outstanding herd sires have evolved from the Patterson ranch.

Today, llamas exist the world over — in Great Britain, Canada, Australia and Europe. Recently Hawaiians have acquired llamas, and New Zealand is considering them as a new source of wool. Even with import bans and a slow start, the number of llamas in the U.S. has multiplied greatly. By spring of 1990, the estimated llama population in this country was 25,000. Prices for llamas have also seen a tremendous escalation. In 1975, females (usually more valuable in any livestock industry) would sell for $1,000. In 1990, the average price range for a female was $10,000 to $20,000.

Zamfir, one of the outstanding herd sires at Big Trees Llama Farm, Valley Ford, California. *Courtesy of Jim and Beula Williams.*

In the background for so many centuries, llamas are now recognized as valuable, utilitarian, and fascinating animals. Much of their popularity is due to their value as pets. With the urbanization of the United States has come a push to suburbia and a resurgence of a "back to nature" philosophy. Individuals and families want pets. Many of these individuals have never owned livestock before and feel intimidated by horses and cattle. For them, llamas are the perfect answer. One llama needs five percent of the space necessary for a horse. Since camelids are hardy, their requirements are less than those of other livestock. One does not have to shoe hooves and the feeding schedule is less regimented.

Their docile and gentle nature make the llamas nonthreatening and safe around small children. Most important, their intelligence, curiosity and even temperament make llamas wonderful companions to owners of all ages and abilities. I have seen people in wheelchairs walking llamas, and handicapped children ably handling their woolly buddies.

In addition, llamas are widely recognized as the ideal wilderness packing companion. Hardy, surefooted and docile, they are tractable enough for even the inexperienced to handle. Llama wool is gaining popularity with home spinners and weavers, and shows with both conformation and performance classes have added to the enjoyment of llamas as a hobby.

REGISTRIES AND ORGANIZATIONS

The oldest llama registry was founded in 1979 by Averill Hyder Abbott as the American Llama Club; her research constituted an attempt to avoid inbreeding and document parentage. In 1982 the International Llama Association was formed and incorporated a registry called CIS, Camelid Identification System.

With Similar goals in mind, the Llama Association of North America (LANA), formed in 1981, backed a Llama Tattoo Registry (LTR) to encourage its membership to put permanent identification marks on all llamas. Naturally, confusion reigned. To simplify matters CIS and LTR merged in 1985 as the International Llama Registry or ILR.

When the two registries merged, the herd records from the Patterson ranch were also incorporated and greatly assisted in documenting the blood lines.

Currently, in order to register a llama, all information known about parents is submitted along with four photos of the llama. Special features, distinct marking and colorations are noted. The ILR highly recommends tattooing the ear. If a llama is tattooed only one photo is required. Another acceptable method of identification involves placing a microchip just under the skin on the left side of the neck. They can be read by a special scanner. In 1991, the registry will close and only llamas whose parents have been previously registered will qualify to be registered, similar to the American Kennel Club (AKC) and other such organizations. Anyone purchasing llamas that have not been registered is encouraged to do so as soon as possible.

Another organization, the American Llama Show Association (ALSA), states that its purpose is to promote the llama throughout America. Its showing mission enhances the visibility of llamas, demonstrates their versatility, establishes showing guidelines, educates and approves show judges, records show points, and awards recognition of champion llamas. ALSA holds clinics throughout the U.S. to train new judges, and a Board of Directors determines eligibility of prospective judges. The association can hold its own shows or sanction those held by other organizations.

CHAPTER TWO

LLAMA TRAITS AND BEHAVIOR

PHYSICAL CHARACTERISTICS

The llama averages four feet at the shoulder and his body is roughly four to five feet long. He comes in many colors ranging from shades of brown through black, red, and white. The body wool is luxuriant and soft, ranging from three to twelve inches in length. He has shorter hair on the face, legs and belly. Whether long or short wool is preferable has long been a controversy. Breeders looking for good pack animals want short wool. If you're interested in spinning and weaving, you probably want a longer-stapled fiber. But the wool is perhaps not nearly as important as the conformation and soundness of the animal; if the llama is unhealthy or knock-kneed, he is useless both as a packer and breeding stock.

There are distinct differences between the llama and the alpaca. Some breeders have tried to increase the woolliness of their llamas by introducing alpaca blood. As a prospective buyer, you need to understand the difference between these two camelids because you will want to know whether you are acquiring an alpaca-llama cross or a pure llama.

Llama ears are generally said to have a definite "banana" shape, whereas the alpaca ear is shorter and stubbier. Recent standards suggest that llama ears do not have to be banana-shaped but should be in proportion and well set on the head.

The llama's tail is about twelve inches in length. The base of the tail on a llama is an extension of the straight line of the back. When the llama is curious, excited or intimidated, he carries the tail in various attitudes. The alpaca's tail base is set lower and appears to blend in with the rump. In addition to these distinctions, in general the alpaca is a smaller animal.

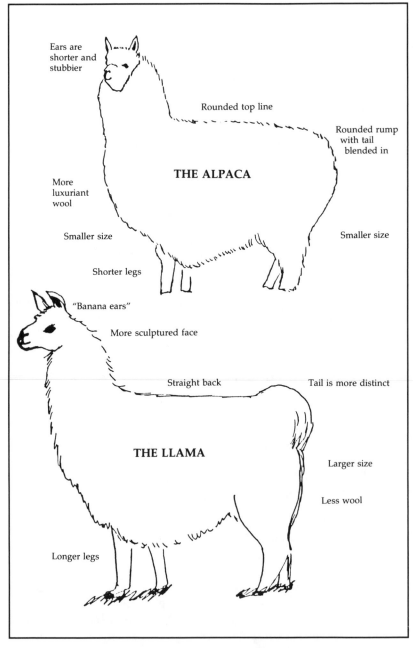

Ears are shorter and stubbier

Rounded top line

Rounded rump with tail blended in

THE ALPACA

More luxuriant wool

Smaller size

Smaller size

Shorter legs

"Banana ears"

More sculptured face

Straight back

Tail is more distinct

THE LLAMA

Larger size

Less wool

Longer legs

Characteristics of the alpaca and the llama.

When a llama is bred with an alpaca, the result is a "huarizo," a lovely combination of long wool and llama characteristics. Unfortunately, such abundant coat decreases in succeeding generations. As a point of interest, in South America the huarizo is considered an accident and candidate for the dinner table!

The llama's eyes are perhaps his most beautiful attribute. Large and fringed by long, sweeping eyelashes, they captivate the beholder. Occasionally, one sees a blue-eyed llama and hears controversy regarding the merit of such pale coloration. Dr. Walter Bravo, DVM, MS, a renowned Peruvian researcher, is very clear that in South America, blue eyes are not a positive trait. South Americans believe the retina in pale eyes can be easily sunburned, especially in areas where it snows and sunlight is more intense.

The split lip found throughout the camel family is a distinctive feature of the llama's face. Watching him nibble and pick through grain with his lips is delightful. Each side of the upper lip can move independently. Thus the lip is like a finger, pressing against the upper gum to pick up the smallest objects. Very seldom do we find strange items in the stomach; the llama is selective and careful. Children love to feel the searching, soft lips on their palms. Since llamas have no upper forward incisors, you needn't worry that they will bite the small hands that feed them.

Like most mammals, llamas have baby teeth and permanent teeth. Around the age of two and a half, most of the baby teeth have fallen out and a new set has grown in. At two to three years, male llamas develop sharp fighting teeth both on the upper and lower jaws. Some adult females also develop them; these teeth should be removed.

Llamas breathe chiefly through their nostrils; that's why you hear so much snorting and sneezing while they eat and play. The llama's neck is long, muscular and quite thin, as you'll discover if you bathe him. In fall, shedding begins around the top of the neck and works gradually down; this is normal.

The llama's body is widest at the chest, tapering down to a small waist line. When we're checking for weight gain, we run our hands along the backbone to feel for the vertebrae. If all we feel is meat, then it's time for a diet! The llama should always be hard and muscular, not flabby.

The llama is a cud-chewing modified ruminant and has three stomach compartments, as opposed to the cow, which has four compartments. Initially when he chews his feed, the llama produces only enough saliva to form a ball or bolus, which he swallows. Later, when he is resting, the bolus is brought or burped back up to be re-chewed,

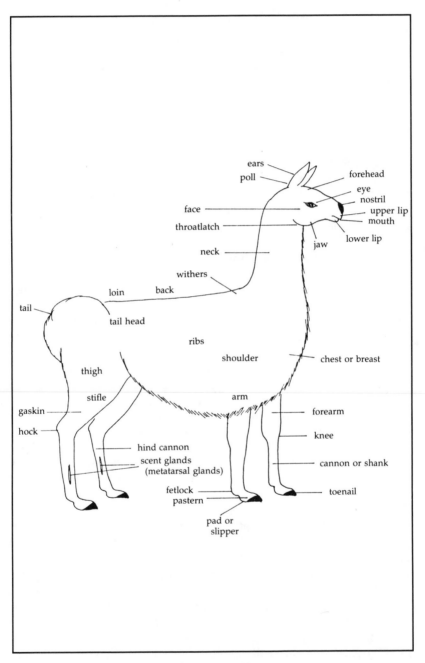

Anatomy of the llama

An alpaca.
*Courtesy of June
Cheny, Truckee-Tahoe
Alpaca Ranch.*

refined and returned to the stomach. In my school visits with llamas, many students have been fascinated to watch that lump move up and down the llama's long neck.

The llama's legs are amazingly functional. Just to watch an animal kneel down, carefully folding in three steps and finally tucking in all the ends, is a study in itself. First, the llama kneels on the forelegs, then sits back on his haunches and finally, with a sigh, settles down in a forward motion on the forelegs. Seated this way, he looks like a sphinx, silent and aloof, chewing his cud. Some llamas will sit starting with the rear legs first!

The llama has indentations approximately four inches long below the hock extending halfway down to the rear foot on both the inside and outside of his rear legs. These look like long scabs, and are metatarsal glands. Those readers familiar with horses may think these are "chestnuts;" however, there is no relationship. Some researchers theorize that the metatarsal glands are scent glands, similar to those of deer. When a llama is excited or alarmed, they emit a slightly musky odor, neither unpleasant nor excessive. This alerts the rest of the herd to danger. There are other scent glands near the toes that are not as obvious.

The llama's foot is designed for hiking and climbing. Two sharp toes dig in and a thick-soled pad grips the trail, similar in effect to snowtires on a four-wheel drive vehicle.

"Touch of Class," an alpaca owned by Alpine Llamas and Alpacas, Jack and Dee Meyer.

Llamas are basically thrifty, healthy animals that can withstand a great variation of feeds and climate.

BEHAVIOR

Whenever we are showing our llamas we are repeatedly asked, "What are their personalities like?" The llama can best be described as intelligent, gentle and extremely inquisitive. Quiet dignity, aloofness and serenity of demeanor all lend to a llama's mystique. Even a newborn cria, whether standing or sitting, will immediately assume a regal posture.

No two llamas' personalities are alike. Some llamas appear to be reserved and wise, while others are bullies and showoffs. In any grouping you will find a leader, a tease, a timid soul, a Huckleberry Finn and a Tom Sawyer. In general, llamas are easy to train, but you must keep the individual personality in mind. Some males can be taught quickly, while others need time to comprehend the task at

Two young males llamas playing.

hand. Some females will be more protective than others, and sires can be either very aggressive while breeding or gentle, almost courtly. Closely observe your llama to determine the training approach that suits him best.

CHARACTERISTICS

In order to better understand the characteristics and behavior of the llama, it is important for the owner to realize that llamas are territorial. Any area allocated by the owner or chosen by the llama, whether it be a corral, feeding area or pasture becomes his protected area. A llama will resent any intrusion into that space by other llamas.

It is believed that this trait is a legacy from their Andean ancestors. In *Llama Medicine*, Stan Ebel relates:

Because of the austere geography and climate of their native Andes, herd survival demanded that territories be carefully

Llamas basking in the sun.

guarded so that no extra animals were admitted. Just one animal beyond the carrying capacity of a territory could spell disaster for most if not all of the herd because of fragile feed supplies. Therefore the territorial male developed an unrelenting aggression toward all invading males, excess breeding females, and weanling-age animals from the production of his own herd. The result of this background and drive is a behavior totally unique to llamas and the other New World camelids. This behavior can be a bit confounding to the novice breeder or uninformed observer.

The stud will proclaim the territory of his herd by marking or defecating along the perimeter. Visiting llamas are challenged, spat upon and physically fought off. Even weanling males are chased away from their own herds.

We can observe this behavior to some degree among the llamas around us. Paradoxically, like other herd animals, the llama feels more comfortable with others of his species around, and will be quite lonesome when by himself. If you plan to buy one llama, buy two! Or quarter him with a sheep, goat, donkey or horse until you acquire a llama companion. This is extremely important, as there have been many sad tales of the "lone llama." Some loners have become aggressive and have had to be put down. Besides, there are few things more enjoyable than watching a couple of llamas play and chase each other around a field.

The herd resembles any normal family. There is the patriarch or senior herd sire, grandmothers, aunts, mothers, sisters and even the kid brothers. Seniority certainly has its privileges, and there are even cliques. Females visiting for breeding are sometimes ostracized until the herd finally accepts them as their own. The least in importance is the last to eat, and curiously, sometimes the sire is the last one allowed at the feed bin.

Pecking order in the herd is easily determined at feeding time. The greenest male or female is at the bottom of the totem pole. As each llama approaches the feeding bin, the current occupant, often the eldest, will lift up his head and pull it backward in a threatening posture, sometimes with a snort or two thrown in. If the intruder persists, then the head is lowered and aimed like a rifle. More snorts, and if that doesn't work, the aggressor will spit in a volley of short, quick blasts.

Llamas tend to be shy and somewhat reserved. Like cats, they come to you when they want to, and catching them in their pen is always a game. At first, they run and cavort until they're cornered. Then with a slight sag in stance, as if they're saying "uncle," they'll give up and permit themselves to be haltered.

Strangers, eager to see these wondrous creatures, often rush up and extend their hands to touch them. The llama's reaction is to take a few steps back, just out of reach, and give the "attackers" a wary eye. It's best to have visitors approach slowly with hands at their sides, and stick out their faces instead. Blowing gently from the lips will often evoke a similar response from the llama, who will take a few steps forward, sniff, and blow back. Llamas greet each other in this manner.

Typically the llama is a hardy animal, and the dam gives birth easily. Mothering comes naturally to the females, and it's rare to have a mother reject her offspring. The new baby, called cria (a shortened version of the Spanish word, "criatura"/infant), is often surrounded by the other herd members, sniffed and welcomed. "How lovely she is!" you can almost hear them murmur.

Communication

The ears, tails and stance are all used in the communication system between llamas. An alert stance with ears up and slightly forward

Llama "body language."

while the tail is up, denotes curiosity: "Something is approaching!" Ears laid back with the tail up says, "Watch out!" If the head is pointing up, and the ears are laid far back against the neck, you had better duck! There's no doubt that somebody is going to get it!

When approached by an older male, young males will assume a crouching position. The head is held low, with the neck down in a "U" shape and the tail folded flat over the back. The ears are tucked back against the neck. This strange stance tells the older male that the young llama is not threatening his harem. But then, in direct contrast, some young males will follow the elder around in the same stance and harass him, nibbling on his legs and sniffing where they shouldn't. It's almost as if they're asking for a fight. Usually the older males are tolerant to a point, then it's time to put the little guy in his place.

Llama sounds are varied, all part of their communication system. As a new llama enters the community area, there is clucking and clicking between the group and the newcomer. One of the most unique sounds is the warble or "orgling" that the male emits when he is either aroused by a passing female, or during breeding. You would think he would become hoarse or have a sore throat after twenty-five to forty-five minutes of orgling.

Most people who listen to a llama hum assume it's content or happy. But if you listen closely, llama hums are distinct: high-pitched and scared, low-pitched and content. When I'm dealing with a frightened animal and I'm scared too, I hum. Together we face the unknown. The llama can feel my strength and my weakness, but more than anything, he needs reassurance, a firm hand and a strong shoulder.

A mother will hum to her baby when she is happy, but the hum becomes high-pitched — a distressed bleat — when he wanders off, or when someone approaches him. There is even a "question mark" hum that ends in a high note when a llama wants to know what's going on in the next stall.

A sound that raises the hair on your neck and quickly gets you out of bed at night is the cry of alarm, which is best described as a donkey's bray. The llama inhales and exhales quickly in short, high-pitched loud cries, telling the herd that something is amiss. There will be no confusion. You'll know when you hear it, and you should check the grounds immediately. Many times, we have leaped from bed only to find a neighbor's cow wandering along the fence, but loose dogs or predators can quickly devastate your herd, so don't take the chance of ignoring an alarm call.

Becoming attuned to these methods of communication will help you understand your animals' moods, and walking through the barn to listen closely will alert you to whether or not all is well.

Caution and Curiosity

When placed in a new area, llamas are extremely cautious, and proceed to carefully sniff and poke around. They never seem to barge into unfamiliar territory without reconnoitering first. In marked contrast to llamas' caution is their overwhelming curiosity. Often, while I'm cooking dinner, a doe-eyed visitor has ambled into the kitchen on quiet feet to critique the evening's menu, nibbling on a few houseplants along the way. Satisfied that I'm doing a good job as dietician, the llama continues her visit into the living room, where she will occasionally sit down, sigh, and watch television.

Anything new is an adventure to a llama, whether it is going on a walk, hiking or jogging. They observe all their surroundings, sometimes stopping and staring intently at some creature in the brush. Along the trail, they'll hum with interest, and grab a few bites of foliage. This curiosity is as prevalent at home; whenever my husband, Don, repairs the barn, he jokingly refers to the herd as his building inspectors. Every new wall, stall, fence, trough and feeder is sniffed, nudged, tasted and otherwise checked out.

Llamas will also rush up to dogs and cats to investigate them, and are inevitably curious about small children. Losing all shyness, they will often walk over to a toddler and take a sniff.

LLAMA VICES

Spitting

The llama's tendency to spit has been somewhat overemphasized and has given llamas a bad name. Llamas meet invasion by spitting. A female will usually "spit off" the male if she is pregnant. It's her way of telling him not to bother her, and breeders use this as an indicator of pregnancy. A frightened or injured llama will spit off its assailant, medical assistant or trainer. Young males in play will chase each other around the field, squealing and taking turns spitting. When a llama does spit, he spreads green flakes and saliva over the victim. The nose will point up and the ears flatten against the neck as a warning. If the invasion continues the llamas will spit a warning volley into the air. The next volley is directed at the invader. The

"This is just a mild warning!"

"Now, I'm getting serious!!!"

Spitting. Before. . . .

After. . . . .

smell is quite offensive to the recipient and to others who happen to be within range. A spit-upon llama will rub his face in the grass, stand around with a hangdog look, and hold his mouth open in a bizarre grimace.

The usual example of dominance in a herd situation is spitting at the feed trough. For this reason many breeders use feeders that prevent the llama from raising its head. While females resolve the dispute, male behavior may escalate to physical contact including ramming of breast bones, biting and kicking.

A well-trained llama doesn't spit, at least not at his handler. Putting a handkerchief over his nose and tying the ends to the halter so that the llama has to endure the odor is one way to break him of this habit. Another device is to use the age-old water pistol accompanied by a firm "No!"

During a recent wildlands fire, we had to evacuate our herd to the local fairgrounds. A llama was brought in by the Sheriff's posse and we were asked to unload and monitor him. Since our llamas are trained not to spit, we were totally unprepared for the sight that greeted us. It was growing dark, but we were still able to see the young gelding lashed to the inside of a large stock trailer. We thought the trailer was painted green inside, only it wasn't paint! His rescuers wore green uniforms, and he was frothing green around his mouth and chin.

Talking softly, Don entered the trailer carrying a halter and lead rope. He was promptly covered in green slime. After a lot of screaming, coaxing and pulling, the llama was finally settled in a stall. He continued to spray anyone that came into range. At first, we attributed this behavior to the terrible ordeal he had been through. But after a few days, we were convinced he was doing it for attention. A lone llama with his own field, he had previously acquired a reputation for spitting at visitors. Our own llamas barely tolerated him, and gave him looks that neighbors might give a spoiled child.

Then one morning, as I was watering our herd, a tired and dirty firefighter wandered over from the Division of Forestry camp to see the llamas. When we approached the visiting gelding's stall, I suddenly remembered what might happen. But it was too late: green spittle rolled down the firefighter's bright yellow poncho. Embarrassed and somewhat peeved, I raised my hose, aimed and fired away. The expression on the gelding's face was comical; here was a human that spit back! He quickly retreated to a back corner of his stall and nursed his pride. On two more occasions I gave him the same treatment, and was happy to turn him over to his owner a few days later a better behaved critter.

Berserk Male Syndrome

One highly debated issue in the llama industry is how much to handle a young cria, male or female. To understand the debate, and to make a sound purchase of your first llama, you need to become familiar with a condition called Berserk Male Syndrome or BMS. If a young male, particularly one less than a month old, has been bottle-fed, isolated from its herd and excessively handled, there is a great danger that the cria has imprinted on humans and identifies with them instead of with his own species. As male crias raised in this manner mature and their testosterone level increases, they will instinctively drive humans from their territory with the same aggressive behavior they would normally direct at invading males. I have seen only one berserk male, and it was a saddening experience. The llama screamed constantly, running up and down the fenceline and spitting at all intruders. He had to be euthanized, as he was miserable and a danger to everyone.

BMS does not manifest until the llama is full grown, at about three years of age. Other symptoms may foreshadow BMS: a very pushy llama will shove or even butt you with his chest; he will play with you like he does with his herd peers.

Thus, at birth, it is extremely important that the young llama identify with its mother and there be no confusion about who is doing the nurturing. In the early days of the llama industry in this country, owners liked to cuddle their woolly crias and sometimes were eager to step in too quickly to assist the dam with a bottle and nipple. As time and experience taught the dangers of BMS, owners became aware of such problems and adopted something of a "hands-off" policy.

Bottlefed females also can become pushy and spitty. If your bottlefed cria is male, he must be neutered as soon as possible, definitely before six months of age. Usually gelding the llama will alleviate the problem, since the testosterone level will be reduced when the testicles are removed, but it is not a guarantee.

Responsible breeders are aware of the problem and avoid bottle-feeding if at all possible. Breeders geld bottlefed males and fully disclose that the cria was raised in this manner to the prospective purchaser. If you are buying your first llama, ask the breeder about the cria's history.

In many respects the danger of BMS in a normal nursing cria is overrated. Young llamas will be curious about you and visitors, and approach cautiously in order to inspect everyone. This is certainly not a signal of future aggression. We do not bring our crias into the house unless it is an emergency. They may wander up on the deck and peer through the glass. We occasionally let our adults meander through the house.

When we are in the barn, we will run our hands along a young male's back and neck, talking softly. This accustoms him to our touch and our tone of voice. We don't hug or fuss excessively; it's more a casual encounter. I do hug the young females now and then, as it's hard not to. We halter both male and female young llamas around four to five months, before weaning and in the presence of the dam.

Don't underrate the danger of BMS, as it can happen. However, don't let the fear of it deter you from owning llamas! A properly raised cria is a source of joy for years to come, and more than likely you'll never encounter a true case of Berserk Male Syndrome.

LLAMA IDIOSYNCRACIES

The Dung Pile

Llamas are naturally housebroken. They can safely be trailered in a carpeted van as they are reluctant to defecate or urinate in unmarked areas. Outdoors, they gravitate to their dung pile when the need arises. Then a curious thing happens; when one relieves itself, the others follow in a chain reaction. The llamas have several dung piles, which makes cleanup easy. When entering a new pen, males will quickly find their spot and mark their territory.

When traveling to shows or transporting llamas long distances for breeding, exercising the llama in "unmarked" territory can be a problem. So, on long trips, we carry a few of the "raisin" pellets in a tupperware container to encourage them along the roadway. They will sniff the container, wiggle their lips in a chewing motion, assume a squatting position, and soon you can be on your way again.

Once as we were returning from the LANA Expo in Vancouver, Washington, we forgot this essential item. We chose a quiet rest area along Highway 5 and let our llama meander around at the end of his lead rope. Nothing! Then we remembered the green astro turf we had used in the stall at the Expo. It was a brilliant idea! We scooped up a few pellets for the remainder of the trip.

The Dust Bowl

Like other animals, llamas love to roll in grass, new straw, and especially dirt! By rolling in the dust bowl, llamas fluff their coat for better insulation. The fine dust helps to keep the wool water repellant. Pregnant females roll more as they near parturition. Old timers say

Rolling in dust bowl.

the dams are positioning the cria. When we open new fields to the herd and the grass is everywhere, one venturesome llama will pick out an area, paw at the spot, and proceed to flatten the grass. The others quickly come along and take turns rolling until the grass is gone and the dust is flying.

When we first began to show llamas, we spent hours shampooing, brushing and drying a pure white llama for her debut. At the end of the day her coat was a dazzling white. As soon as we released her, Snow Princess made a beeline for the dust bowl. Within seconds, she was a brown llama. We have since learned to groom, especially white llamas, at the last possible moment before a show; afterwards, we keep them confined on clean straw.

Dancing

When the weather is changing, a wind is coming up or sometimes at dusk, a curious thing happens. Once you see it, you'll never forget it. We call it llama dancing. One llama begins a lazy gallop, quickly followed by another and another until they are all in a line, one behind the other. Then with a silent signal, the gallop becomes a springing. Their legs look like pogo sticks as they bounce straight up in the air,

Llamas visiting Convelescant Hospital. *Courtesy of Betty Barkman.*

and continue around and around the field. Our whole family gathers, laughing and pointing to our nymphs of the evening. In the gathering dusk, there is no sound but the gentle pounding of padded feet. They look so comical and yet regal, we can only marvel at this fascinating behavior.

THE "PR" LLAMA

We take our llamas to public schools for demonstrations, where they'll wander around the classroom sniffing at tousled heads, desks and displays. Teachers are always amazed at the good manners of these woolly guests. One day when I had taken a llama to my daughter's class I released the lead rope and let him wander around. There were several models of old Spanish missions on the floor which the students had spent many hours building. As the llama approached them we all held our breath; he gingerly set his feet down between the delicate miniature walls and "haciendas" until he found a place to "kush" (take a seat)!

Every Christmas a dedicated group of about three hundred people who call themselves "The Joy of Giving" gather at one of the local convalescent homes. The group splits up and visits all the rest homes in the area. Five Santa Clauses distribute gifts donated by the local merchants to the patients.

On Christmas Day 1989 I was asked to add a llama to the festivities. Since he is our most mellow, Grey Fox was nominated for the task. I had planned to have him carry a pack but rejected that idea when I realized he would have to maneuver between beds. Instead, we placed a Santa Claus hat with holes for the ears on his head. Around his neck was a huge red bow. We had to tie the hat to his head so he wouldn't remove it as he had to enter and exit the van so many times.

When we arrived at the first convalescent home, the patients were lined up in the lobby wheelchair to wheelchair. Everyone began to laugh, point and clap. Sedately and regally, Grey Fox took center stage. Not wanting to completely upstage the real Santa Claus, I latched on to one of the nurses and asked her to guide us to the rooms where the bed-ridden patients were.

We went down the halls from room to room. Grey Fox would gingerly walk up to the beds and quizzically blow into each person's face. Some would awaken, startled, and then smile broadly. Others opened their mouths into the biggest "O's" I have ever seen. Tentative hands would reach out and stroke the soft wool of his neck. If the patients moved too quickly, the llama would step back slightly, but most of the time he stood quietly.

As he approached the bed in one room, he glanced to the side, stopped and stared. I looked over to see what fascinated him, and saw a large mirror. Cautiously, he walked up to his own image and blew into the glass. The patient was delighted by this odd behavior.

An elderly woman in another room exclaimed that she had never seen a llama in all her ninety-two years. But the most memorable moment came near the end of our visit. In this room, family members and a nurse were attending to a patient who appeared to be oblivious to all activity around her. When we entered and walked up to her bedside, she raised her head and said, "Oh my, a llama!" Everyone around me seemed amazed. I didn't understand the sudden commotion until the nurse explained to me that the woman hadn't spoken a word for six months until that moment.

Grey Fox and I made the rounds of all the hospitals that day. At each stop I took him for a walk to relieve himself, carrying along a

"Bah-Humbug"

few llama pellets in a container to remind him. We started at 9:00 a.m. and didn't finish until 2:00 p.m. Grey Fox never tired, and greeted the front door of each hospital as a new challenge.

For two days after Christmas, I received phone calls from relatives and staff thanking me for bringing my llama Santa Claus. A physical therapist called after the third day to tell me that nothing had made such a stir in the wards as the llama. The patients were still talking about the magical grey llama that came to visit on Christmas day. Some even said he was a giant toy that I had wound up and made walk!

CHAPTER THREE

ACQUIRING A LLAMA

So you've caught "the bug" and decided to buy llamas. Where do you go? What do you look for? Years ago, buyers of exotic animals went to zoos, hoping to purchase their surplus. Today there are many llama breeders, individuals with animals to sell, and auctions where llamas are put up for bid.

Before you even begin to search for llamas that are for sale, the wise course of action is to examine your needs, facilities, and abilities and attempt to match them with the right animals.

First, consider how you plan to use your llamas: for packing, as unique pets, to breed, as the foundation for a herd, etc.

The use will often determine which sex you should consider. For example, if you plan to pack or drive llamas, or keep them as backyard pets, geldings are by far the best choice. If you plan to keep more than two animals to use, with no desire to breed, again geldings are your choice. You can pasture several geldings together, and if you later decide to get into breeding, they will not present problems to either sex of unneutered llamas, and generally get along well with weanling crias.

On the other hand, if you decide you want to breed on a limited scale, young female crias may best fit your needs and your pocketbook.

If you are experienced with livestock and have the facilities, starting a herd with a potential or proven sire and several females may be your choice.

When purchasing your first animals, the advantages of buying trained adult llamas are attractive to new owners who lack time and patience. But the special bonding of young llamas with their trainer, the joys of accomplishment and just plain "growing up together" may have greater appeal. In any event, the mature llamas can learn to trust you just as well.

Price is another consideration. Trained pack geldings are currently selling in a range of $1000 to $1500. A weanling male suitable for

Herd of dams and crias resting.

gelding (six months to one year) or a young untrained gelding you can train yourself will bring $600 and up. Bred adult females range in price from $10,000 to $20,000. Female crias, depending upon quality and pedigree, sell for $7500 to $10,000, while proven studs go from $5000 to upwards of $100,000.

WHERE TO FIND YOUR LLAMA

A variety of people advertise or put the word out on the grapevine that they have a llama for sale. But be aware of potential problems; some people may have acquired llamas as a hobby or on a whim, only to have the fun wear off after a few months. Lacking the time to properly care for and train their pets, they now want to move on to a different hobby. These animals may have been spoiled or neglected; some may have developed habits that warrant an experienced handler's correction. Therefore, when you approach a private seller, ask such questions as "Why are you selling your llama?" "Were your

Two crias check out the author's camera.

males bottle-fed?" In the case of the lone llama, you'll want to ask, "At what age was he separated from the herd?" "Is he pushy?" "Is he difficult to handle?" "May I call you later with my questions?"

While it is important to be alert to the pitfalls of buying a llama from a private owner, do not discount the amateur breeder altogether, as you can often purchase an excellent animal this way.

By far the most popular way to acquire a llama is to visit breeders in your area or to contact llama ranchers in other states. In order to obtain names of breeders, write to the Llama Association of North America (LANA) or the International Llama Association (ILA) and ask for a breeder's list. You might want to join such an organization for the wealth of information to be gained from newsletters, pamphlets and other publications (see appendix).

Breeders are generally happy to have you visit and are eager to share their enthusiasm for this marvelous species. Most will give you excellent advice and be available should you have questions after your purchase. Many lasting friendships have begun with a visit to a llama ranch.

A third alternative in the acquisition of a llama is to contact a broker or go to an auction. For the novice, buying at an auction can be very risky. If you are unfamiliar with llamas and uncertain of what constitutes good conformation or soundness, you can get caught up in the excitement and pay more than you would have through private treaty. It is vital to preview all prospects and study each animal's background. Then, with an appropriate price in mind, enter the ring! If bidding exceeds your limit, stop, and wait for the next time. Many fine llamas have been acquired through auctions. But, it is best to either have some experience or take·an experienced breeder with you.

A final way to buy a llama is to respond to an advertisement. The llama publications listed in the appendix have classified sections and display ads by llama breeders. The International Llama Association and the Llama Association of North America also send newsletters to their members which include classified ad sections listing animals for sale. Subscribing to various publications will keep you updated on shows and sales, and by attending county and state fair llama exhibits you can meet various breeders and contestants who have animals available.

VISITING A BREEDER

Once you are armed with lists and maps, you're ready to hit the road. Call first to make an appointment. This is a courtesy that will be appreciated and the professional breeder will want to have time to proudly show you his herd and thoroughly answer your questions.

When you've reached your destination, look the premises over. Are they clean and well-organized? Do the animals look healthy and sound? Does the owner seem knowledgeable? The more ranches you visit, the more insight you will gain. You will notice different methods of fencing, housing and breeding; take notes to check against your reservoir of information or to review with an experienced llama owner. Visit a number of breeders and learn about different types and bloodlines. Take some time before making any purchasing decision.

Some breeders may have mature stock for sale, while others will have crias for sale at a later date. As both good and bad points may be inherited by the offspring, ask to see both your prospect's sire and dam. If neither one is available, carefully review a photograph.

If you want a cria from a particular female, you may be asked to put down a deposit to hold it. Crias can be weaned at five to six months. We recommend that purchasers wait two to three weeks after weaning before taking delivery. Thus the shock of separation from the dam isn't compounded by a trip to a new home.

Good front structure.

EXAMINING THE INDIVIDUAL

When you have found a likely prospect, keep the following points in mind:

1. Is the llama healthy and sound? His eyes should be clear and sparkling, and his coat soft and lustrous. As diarrhea can indicate illness or worms, the llama's feces should be in the form of shiny, round and compact pellets. A healthy llama is alert and curious.

2. Does the animal have good conformation? His back should be straight, with no hump or sag. His legs should be straight, fore and aft. Avoid an animal with knock-knees, cow-hocks, sickle-hocks or bowed legs. If he has extremely long wool, ask the owner to wet the legs down so that you can check them.

Good rear structure.

Optimally, his ears should be somewhat banana-shaped. He should have an overall, well-balanced look that is pleasing to the eye.

3. How is your prospect's temperament? He should be moderately shy and wary. Do his parents have good dispositions? Observe his interaction with the rest of the herd. Young llamas should join in easily with the herd. Teenagers will play with one another, nibbling on each other's legs, and butting one another's chests. Young males and females will indiscriminately mount their dams; their curiosity is like a magnet, drawing them together and toward you. Do not confuse curiosity with aggressiveness. Some young crias will sniff you all over and tip-toe behind you to get a whiff of your clothing. When you turn and reach out to touch him, your investigator will swiftly take flight. An aggressive llama will attempt to shove you; he should be avoided.

A young cria with good overall conformation and balance.

4. A cria in particular should be up to date on its vaccinations; try to obtain copies of the records for your veterinarian's file. Before you buy a cria, be sure that it is halter-broken for ease of handling. If you risk purchase of a cria that has not been trained to lead, you may find him difficult to load and transport safely.

If you are interested in breeding, ask about the animal's bloodlines and whether or not the sire and dam are related. If the llama is registered, request a copy of the papers.

In checking the registration of your prospective llama, you can determine whether either parent has been designated as alpaca, and whether or not your candidate for purchase is a "huarizo."

If you are uncertain about the animal's health or conformation, have your veterinarian do a pre-purchase exam at your expense. This is a common and wise practice for both novice and experienced llama buyers.

TAKING YOUR LLAMA HOME

You can haul llamas young and old in a van, a pickup truck with stock racks, or a trailer. Even large adult llamas will fit in a standard van. During our recent wildlands fire evacuation, I had five adult females in our standard van. That's too many for a long trip!

Llamas will rarely defecate in a van, but you may want to line the floor with indoor-outdoor carpeting or similar material. We lay down a plastic tarp and then cover it with carpeting for better traction.

If you use a pickup, be sure that the sides are high enough to prevent the llama from jumping over. If you use a standard horse or stock trailer, DO NOT tie the animal with his lead rope, as he could slip and fall, and hang himself. Many a sad story has been told of llamas found dead at the end of a trip from broken necks and suffocation.

On long trips we stop every two to three hours to give our occupants a breather, a chance to relieve themselves (if we are using the van) and to see if all is well in the back. In hot weather, we water each animal.

If you are using a trailer in cold weather, take the wind-chill factor into consideration. When traveling in cold weather at 55 miles per hour, the trailer temperature drops dramatically. Close open windows and give your llama extra protection. Even the floors should be covered with a mat or pad, since the llama tends to lie down once the journey is underway. There is very little fleece on the underside of the animal; thus cold penetrates easily. As a rule, we avoid transporting llamas in a trailer during extreme cold, preferring the warm van instead.

CHAPTER FOUR

FACILITIES

When we purchased our first llamas, "Cheech" and "Chong," a handsome pair of males, we frantically built a corral using round posts and three rails to enclose roughly half an acre around our rear deck. Our neighbors, horse people, commented that this enclosure was durable and should work well.

While our family waited to see the exotic creatures that were to so completely transform our lives, we unloaded and turned the llamas into the corral and went to relax admiringly on the deck. They wandered around their new quarters, scrutinizing and sniffing every board and rail.

Suddenly, there was dead silence. Very carefully, Cheech poked his head between the rails and lifted one foreleg and then the other over. Then he squeezed the rest of his body through like a tube of toothpaste. He was LOOSE!

We sailed over the rails of our deck and ran for the open field, circling the llama. Trapped and unwilling to leave his companion, Cheech hovered by the fence. Don quickly knocked down the rails so that the llama could go back in. Once he was confined we reinforced the corral with woven wire nailed to the rails (field fencing), and this is what we use today.

PLANNING YOUR FACILITIES

Llamas are extremely agile and, especially when young, may crawl under a rail fence. Before you begin building your enclosure, develop a plan. Decide what to use for the perimeter and for cross-fencing. We have found that you can comfortably have five llamas per acre. Maybe you're only planning on having a pair. More likely, you'll acquire additional animals at a later date. Take these factors into account as you formulate your plan.

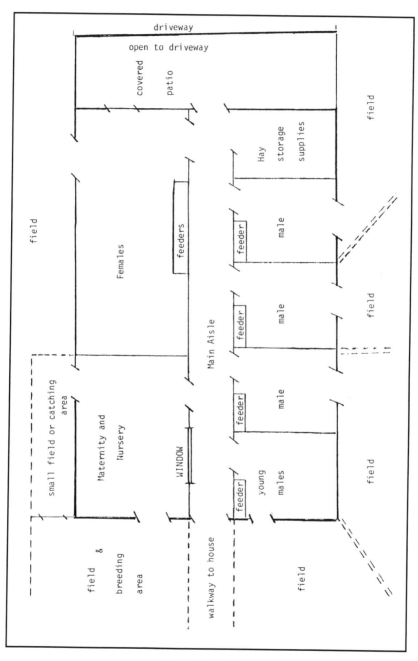

Barn floor plan

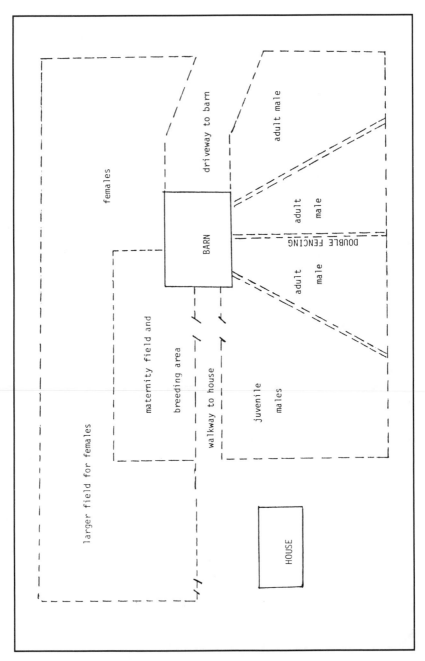

A sample layout for barn and corrals.

Weanlings will have to be separated from their dams and never placed with larger males, since a 300 lb. llama can harm a smaller youngster while only playing. Never keep weanling females with intact adult males or you will invite unwanted pregnancy and injury. You'll need a separate area for breeding (the other "bachelors" can get very jealous). We have often found it necessary to move fences so that routine management such as breeding did not disrupt the rest of our herd. By thinking ahead, you'll save yourself a lot of work.

If you plan a full-scale llama operation and to own more than one herd sire, separate them. Some owners do confine breeding males in the same pasture, but in such instances, you'll need at least five acres so that each can mark his own territory. If you keep them in adjoining corrals, put double fencing between them. Breeding males screech at one another, and generally carry on in a macho manner to impress feminine onlookers. As a rule, geldings don't exhibit this behavior.

The solitary herd sire can be kept with pregnant females, but I do not recommend this practice; pregnant llamas can abort at any time and be re-bred. Months later you will realize that your dam isn't overdue but began a late gestation. Crias may be accidentally bred as early as five months.

Assessing your acreage in terms of how many llamas you think you might acquire will help you determine your course of action. Visiting others' llama ranches may provide you with a range of options.

Before you begin fencing, double-check your property line. If you live in a high fire danger area, allow for a firebreak from the property line to the fence. Get your plan down on paper, drawing gates and barn access. Allow for a holding pen, feeding areas and delivery access. You'll need to be able to enter each field with a large truck; someday you may have to remove a sick llama or bring in a tractor. Plan gates and cross-fencing for rotating pastures.

In planning your pastures be sure that protection areas are accessible to all your stock. Llamas do not need elaborate shelter; in normally mild climates a three-sided shed is sufficient. They do need shade in spring and summer, and protection from winter wind. It is easy to overlook the wind chill factor; many llamas have incurred frostbite on their ears.

FENCING

A four-foot fence is adequate for most llamas, but some have jumped these. Five or six foot heights are preferable. There are many kinds of suitable fencing with varying costs; research your local farm outlets and fence companies before you build.

The wooden rail fence with wood posts will last a long time, particularly if you use pressure-treated posts. Normal wood will rot from the moisture in the ground after a few years; pressure-treated wood is creosoted to deter wood-destroying organisms.

You can paint the aesthetically pleasing rails your favorite color, but maintaining the paint job can be tiresome. The rails for a corral for breeding males should be set higher and closer together to prevent nipping.

Field fencing wire has smaller squares at the bottom and larger ones at the top. A disadvantage of field fencing is that it can stretch; it eventually starts drooping and loses its straight line. Secure it with metal "T" posts pounded into the ground. The sharp top edges of the "T" posts can be covered with caps. Corner posts should be wooden and cemented in. Bury the bottom edge of the fence approximately six inches to discourage stray dogs and predators from burrowing under.

Electric fence is very successful and surprisingly inexpensive. Llamas quickly learn their boundaries with this system. There are many kinds, requiring various methods of installation. One of these is the New Zealand fence which consists of several wires and wood posts; this lasts a long time and is popular with larger llama ranchers.

Poly vinyl chloride (PVC) pipe rail fencing is latest on the market. Consisting of lightweight hollow core tubing, it is durable and non-chewable. It is currently available only in white and never needs painting. Although it costs more to buy and install, it requires minimal maintenance.

If you don't plan to develop a large herd, you might want to investigate chain link fence with a top rail. The bottom can be buried below ground level, and you will have a *secure* fence. Though expensive, it is one of the best forms of fencing for small areas.

I know of no llama owner who either recommends or uses barbed wire. If you have ever seen a deer, cow or horse that has become entangled in barbed wire, you will never forget it. Whatever fence you choose, make a habit of walking fencelines regularly. Check for burrow-holes, loose posts and missing connectors. Llamas are playful, and can unwittingly take advantage of weak fencing.

New Zealand high tensil electric fencing.

Cross fencing at Llama Llegends, Sonny and Sue Rodgers,
Nevada City, California

A solar powered electric gate is inexpensive but very effective.

Loafing or day shed.

SHELTERS

Shelter for your llamas can be as simple as a three-sided shed or as deluxe as an elaborate barn, depending on climate and pocketbook. In any event, it is most important to offer protection from the elements. An octagonal structure and barn setup are pictured in the following pages. The 4'x 8' plywood panels of the octagonal shed can be nailed to the side supports during winter and removed during summer. You can fence all the way to the center support so that the shed becomes the nucleus of four corrals.

A barn works well for many breeders and is easily adapted to individual circumstance. Males are separated from females and allowed minimal eye contact. The younger males may observe the breeding pen and learn from their elders. Our barn has open stalls, an aisleway and a completely enclosed stall which we call the nursery or maternity room. This area has insulated walls, raised flooring and an easily regulated, safe heater. Hanging scales, medical supplies and a restraining apparatus are readily accessible. The latter is simply a 6-ft. long metal gate attached near the corner of the stall. We can confine a female between the gate and parallel wall to check her milk production, or palpate her in the event of an emergency.

The nursery should have a window on the aisle so you can observe the newborn cria without interrupting the bonding process. Make it easy to direct your flashlight into the stall through this window.

The males' stalls are high-sided with rigid 2" x 6" boards between individual pens. The females are generally kept in a herd with access to a large pasture and a covered area for bad weather. If the females' pastures borders the "maternity" area, they can observe the new mother and her cria.

INTRODUCING THE NEW ARRIVAL

Whenever you bring a new llama onto your property or into an existing herd, quarantine the newcomer for approximately thirty days. This may seem cruel, since he or she will be lonely during this time. However, you need such an interlude for a veterinary check and to observe the animal for contagious disease. The new llama can familiarize himself with the surroundings without incurring the harassment of curious companions.

Once you're satisfied that your new llama is healthy, gradually mainstream him into your group. Your herd will cluck and click as it

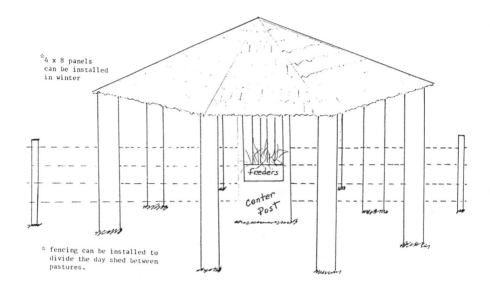

An octagonal day shed can be the hub or core of
two or more separate corrals.

checks the intruder out; even the crias will be very interested. Remain
with the group for about an hour until everyone loses interest and
begins to graze.

Your newcomer may be ostracized at feeding time, even to the
point of being spit upon and chased away from the feeder. Don't be
alarmed; he will have to learn the group's pecking order and gradually
assert his position. You may want to feed him away from the others
for several days for your own peace of mind.

Most other livestock intermingle well with llamas, but be cautious.
We don't stable our horse with the llamas because we are afraid she
might kick one of our females in a power struggle over feed. Their
pastures and stalls are adjacent.

Some horses panic when confronted with their first llama. Once
when Don was walking El Cid down the road near our neighbor's
house, their newly acquired horse took one look, sailed over the fence
and vanished into the horizon. It took hours to recover him. Whenever
we participate in a parade, we always ask for a position a good distance
from any equine units. Such fearful reactions are not always the case,
as we have had several friends visit on horseback without incident.

Be prepared, and go slowly to see how the horse reacts to your llamas; pasture them apart until they're used to each other.

Goats socialize well with llamas. As goats butt anything and everything (even pygmy goats' horns can be sharp), have them dehorned. We pasture our goats and llamas together; their antics at feeding time are hysterical. It's amazing how a two-foot-tall billy can intimidate a llama that towers over him. We confine our geese to their own area; if you've ever owned a flock, you know how aggressive they can be, especially if some are nesting. Their wings are powerful, and they can give an inquisitive cria a nasty bite on the nose.

We keep our dog separated from new livestock, including llamas, for several days and let him know by our care and feeding that the newcomer belongs. When the dog's interest wears off, we know he has accepted his new charge.

The practice on our ranch is not to allow our guard dog to run with the llama herd. He has a perimeter run of the territory without access to the inner pens. Many ranches have guard dogs that do run with the herd and such a practice has worked well for them.

Whether or not you allow your dog to be with your llamas should depend on his training and temperament. Problems quickly arise

Llamas are curious about other pets.

when other dogs visit and engage in pack behavior by chasing your llamas. Like any gang situation, this quickly gets out of hand, and your animals can be injured or killed. Sad stories abound of how the family house dog got carried away when joined by other dogs and killed a llama.

Cattle can be put in with llamas, but I don't recommend it; cows and steers are hosts to numerous internal parasites. Since they defecate all over a pasture, as opposed to the llamas' central dung pile, your llama can easily acquire a case of worms.

Whatever your decisions are about fencing, housing, other livestock and protection of your llamas, know that you have many options, and can profit from the experience of breeders in your area.

CHAPTER FIVE

LLAMA NUTRITION

Nutrition is one of the most controversial topics in the llama industry. What do you feed them, how much, and at what times of the day? When we first began our operation, everyone we knew fed alfalfa and various forms of grain. We believed that the more we fed them, the healthier they would be.

There have been sweeping changes in this philosophy. Today, researchers are specializing in llama nutrition; large llama ranches have conducted studies and compiled information. This transformation began because breeders saw increased percentages of bone deformities and breeding and birth problems. We now know, for example, that obesity in the llama is one of the primary causes of premature births and failure to lactate. When the animal is too fat, there is little room for fetal development or milk production.

Llamas are browsers, meandering around a pasture and taking a bite here and there. A llama can only consume 1.8% of its body weight in dry matter, and approximately one-third of its daylight hours are spent grazing. The remaining time is for rest and cud-chewing.

NUTRITIONAL COMPONENTS

Protein and Fiber

Protein is necessary for energy. Llamas and other camelids digest protein and fiber more efficiently than their ruminant cousins. Protein levels should be between ten and sixteen percent of the total diet (lower percentages for less active animals). Some hay suppliers provide chemical hay tests to assess percentages of protein, moisture content, and nutrients. If your supplier doesn't do this, ask him where you can have it analyzed. When buying grain, look on the tags or on the bag for a content analysis.

Crucial to the diet, fiber encourages stomach compartments and the gastrointestinal tract toward maximum function. Ideally, twenty-

"Dinner anyone?"
Calvin Klein, Llasa
Llama Ranch.

five percent of intake should be fiber. Forages will vary in the amounts of fiber, and you should feed high fiber levels.

Minerals

Exact mineral requirements for the llama have not been determined, but owners and researchers have looked to the needs of other livestock (cattle and sheep) for guidance.

Selenium — This mineral is a very important for livestock. The amount present in hay is determined by where it is grown. Some parts of the country have high selenium content in the soils and other areas are deficient.

Selenium in excess is toxic, whereas a deficiency can cause reproductive problems, abortions, decreased resistance to disease, and muscle degeneration called White Muscle Disease. Lack of selenium in feed can be rectified with the use of a salt block which contains it as well as other trace minerals. Consult your local veterinarian to determine correct dosages based on weights and activities of your llamas for your area.

WHAT TO FEED

Baled Hay

If you are preparing for your first llamas and have only a small paddock, you will need to find a source of hay. Most feed stores buy hay from different areas of the country, depending on price and availability. You need to know where the hay was grown, as soil determines the percentage of nutrients in forage. Your hay should be free of weeds and thistles.

Alfalfa hay is very high in protein. Llamas love to eat the leaves and will leave the stems for last. Thus, the amount of fiber is reduced. When buying alfalfa hay, keep in mind that whether or not it is first, second, third or fourth cutting determines its percentage of protein. Early cuttings will have higher protein and less fiber than the third and fourth cuttings.

Oat hay has an excellent balance of protein and fiber (but make sure you have a good barn cat to control the mice that love this food source). It is usually readily available from feed suppliers.

Grass hay also is a valuable source of nutrition, but may be difficult to obtain during certain times of the year. We try to stockpile grass hay in early summer when it is more available.

Pelletized Alfalfa

Alfalfa can be dried and compressed with or without grain into pellet form, a feed popular with backpackers for its convenience on the trail. To minimize the possibility that toxic substances (such as poisonous plants) have been incorporated into the feed, make sure that it is supplied by a reliable source, and that the pellets have been analyzed. We feed alfalfa pellets without grain added in order to regulate individual animal's intake. Be careful when feeding your llama pellets, as choking when gorging is a possibility. Spread the pellets out or mix them in with the hay so that the forager has to pick them out.

Grain

Grain comes in many forms — whole oats, rolled oats, bran, corn (whole or cracked) — and can supply increased energy and some protein. However, in many instances grains lack minerals such as calcium and phosphorus. Many owners combine grain with protein supplements, vitamins, and molasses to insure that the llama has a balanced and nutritive diet, or purchase a pelleted complete ration.

3%
salt

45%
fiber

35%
water

5%
vitamin
and
mineral

10%
protein

2%
fat

Percentage of various elements in a well-balanced diet.

Flaked, cracked, or whole corn is one of the best sources of energy. Incidentally, if you can get your hands on dried corn stalks, you'll be supplying a great source of fiber to your llamas. They will strip the cornstalks, making clean up easy.

Whole cottonseed is a concentrate that is well balanced with twenty percent protein, twenty percent energy in fat content, and twenty percent fiber. It's usually only available in large quantities.

Mineral Supplements

Dr. LaRue Johnson of the Colorado State University College of Veterinary Medicine has spent years researching llama nutrition and is considered a leading authority. He has formulated a combination of nutrients which I recommend. The formula is comprised of large amounts so you may want to have your feed supplier mix it for you in smaller quantities.

50 lbs. trace mineralized salt
50 lbs. steamed bone meal
50 lbs. dried powdered molasses
10 lbs. "Zinpro 100"

Water

Water is essential to a llama's survival. It must be available at all times. Llamas suck in the fluid with the mouth slightly opened.

Running streams and ponds are popular drinking sources. Usually llamas are careful not to drink polluted water, but they can acquire *giardia*, a protozoan found in many streams which causes gastrointestinal upset. We supply domestic water. You may observe that pastured llamas don't seem to drink as much because they also derive moisture from the grasses in the pasture. Llamas on dry feed require more water. Normally a 250-pound llama drinks 7.8 liters of water per day.

If you live in cold climates where water freezes, you will need to invest in a stock heater. Be careful; llamas are curious enough to remove them, and heaters can cause a fire if they land in the hay. Secure your heater in the tank and connect it to a grounded outlet with a three-prong grounded plug.

AMOUNTS AND WHEN TO FEED

Here again, circumstances will vary according to what you have available. We feed once a day in the morning. We allow one flake — approximately five inches of a bale — per large animal. Lactating females are supplemented with grain. If we find hay left over the following morning, we cut back slightly until all is consumed. You may have to experiment to arrive at an amount that works.

When you bring home a new llama, keep him on the feed he is used to eating. Change over gradually by mixing old and new feed together for a few days. Avoid drastic changes that might upset his stomach.

Overeating

Like other ruminants, llamas will gorge on grain and treats if given the chance. Always be sure to store all grain, dog food, chicken feed,

Cold weather does not bother llamas if they have a loafing shed
for shelter. Taken at the Dennings ranch, Bishop, California,
by Betty Barkman.

and grass seed away from the herd. Llamas are adept at removing
lids from garbage cans where such items often are stored. It's also
important to keep llamas out of orchards and gardens. Colic can result
from such binges.

Weight Control

The adult llama's weight varies according to bone density and
height. An adult female llama normally weighs from 238 to 441
pounds. Adult males are within a range of 286 to 536 pounds. With
such variation, it is difficult to use weight tables to assess your llama.

To check whether your animals are overweight, look at and man-
ually examine your animal. Four areas give you clues: thighs, ribs,
chest, and vertebrae. Kneel behind your llama so that you are eye-level
with the middle thigh. You should be able to see the female's udder
or the male's penis. Next, walk to your llama's side and place your
hand right behind the top of the foreleg, in the chest area. You should
be able to feel the ribs. Then, facing the llama from the front, look
and feel between the forelegs. Is there fat that jiggles? The last test,

A common type of feeder for a herd.

which is the best, is to part the wool along the topline of the back and run your hand along the vertebrae. You should feel a slightly concave area between the two spines of the vertebrae. If you have ever taken the meat off the neck bone of a chicken, you know that there is a lateral hollow along the vertebrae. If you do not feel the valley or you do not feel the vertebrae at all, you have a fat llama.

Overweight llamas should be taken seriously. Obesity is a major cause of infertility, abortion, premature births, and susceptibility to heat stress. In addition, life expectancy is shortened.

FEEDERS

Llamas protect their eating domain and will spit at other llama intruders. If the head llama decides to eat first, then all the others will have to wait their turn. In order to feed several animals at one time, some llama owners have devised ingenious feeders. Llamas have to raise their heads in order to spit, so some designs have a bar or beam running down the length of the feeder. The llamas have to put their heads under the bar to eat and are prevented from raising them quickly to spit at a neighbor. A design that we are partial to is a long feeder with holes cut in the side. Each llama has his own hole. He must withdraw his head (leaving the food) to spit at a companion.

All feeders should be under cover and out of the elements. Never feed llamas directly off the ground as they can ingest parasites and dirt along with the feed. Salt blocks should also be placed out of the rain and near the feed areas.

Creep Feeders

If an overweight dam has a cria at her side, you have a minor problem. Crias start munching on hay as early as one week of age. Since the cria needs to have forage available, you can't deny him while his dam is on a diet. The creep feeder will solve this problem. Design an enclosure or small fenced area with a separate feeder for the cria. The entrance should be small enough so that the dam cannot enter. Putting a top rail over the entry and a bottom board so that she cannot crawl through usually does the trick. Once you have placed your cria inside, he will get the idea.

POISONOUS PLANTS

Some new owners seem more concerned with weed control than with their llama's nutrition. Since llamas love to browse on bushes and grass, the idea does have merit. But as llamas are picky eaters, and will eat some, but not all weeds, you might end up with a yard that looks moth-eaten. It might be best to settle for a goat that is not so particular when he grazes down your yard. Our pygmy goats do a great job.

Llamas will munch on exotic plants, both at home and on the trail, and some of these can be poisonous. The most commonly found around home are rhododendron, azaleas, and oleander. Don't just fence around them — get rid of them! If a llama ever got loose and decided to nibble, the results could be fatal. Become familiar with poisonous plants in your area and areas where you plan to backpack. Your local agricultural extension agent can help. (For treatment of poisonous plant ingestion, see Chapter 9.)

POISONOUS PLANTS FOUND
ON THE TRAIL AND IN THE PASTURE

Common Name	Scientific Name
African Rue	*Peganum*
Arrowgrass	*Triglochin*
Black Lauren & Mountain Laurel	*Leucothoe Davisiae*
Buckeyes	*Aesculus*
Buttercups	*Ranunculus*
Castor Bean	*Ricinus Communis*
Chokecherry, Wild Cherry	*Prunus Emarginata &*
	Prunus Virginiana
Cocklebur	*Xanthium*
Death Camas, Sandcorn	*Zigadenus*
False Hellebore, Corn Lilly	*Veratrum Californicum*
Fiddleneck	*Amsinckia Intermedia*
Fly poison, Stagger grass,	*Amianthium Muscae Toxicum*
crow poison	
Groundsel	*Senecio Vulgaris*
Greasewood	*Sarcobatus Vermiculatus*
Hemlock, Poison Hemlock,	*Cicuta Maculata &*
Water Hemock	*Conium Maculatum*
Henbane	*Hyoscyamus Niger*
Horsebrush	*Tetradymia*
Indian Hemp	*Cannabis Sativa*
Jimsonweed, Thornapple	*Datura Meteloides &*
	Datura Stramonium
Labrador Tea	*Ledum Glandulosum*
Locoweed	*Astragalus*
Manchineel	*Hippomane Mancinella*
Mandrake and Mayapple	*Mandragora Officinarum &*
	Podophyllum Peltatum
Mesquite	*Prosopis*
Milkweed	*Asclepia*
Mistletoe	*Phoradendron Flavescens*
Mushrooms	*Amanita*
Nightshade	*Solanum*
Oak Brush	*Quercus*
Oleander	*Nerium Oleander*
Pokeweed	*Phytolacca Americana*
Rhododendron	*Rhododendron*
Spurges	*Euphorbia*
Tansy Ragwort	*Senecio Jacobes*
Tobacco Tree, Tobacco	*Nicotiana Glauca*
Western Azalea	*Rhododendron Occidentale*
Western Sneezeweed	*Helenium Hoopesii*

POISONOUS PLANTS FOUND
IN THE GARDEN AND LANDSCAPING

Common Name	Scientific Name
Amaryllis, The Daffodil family	*Amaryllidaceae*
Autumn Crocus	*Colchicum Autumnale*
Azalea	*Rhododendron*
Black Locust Tree	*Robinia Pseudoacacia*
Bleeding Heart	*Dicentra Species*
Box	*Buxus Sempervirens*
Castor Bean Plant	*Ricinus Communis*
Cherry Laurel, Wild Cherries, Wild Plums	*Prinus Caroliniana*
Chinaberry Tree	*Melia Azedarach*
Christmas Rose (False Hellebore)	*Helleborus Niger*
Cyclamen	
Daphne	*Daphne Mezereum*
English Ivy	*Hedra Helix*
Foxglove (Purple Foxglove)	*Digitalis Purpurea*
Gingko Tree	*Gingko Biloba*
Golden Chain Tree	*Laburnum Vulgare Anagyroides*
Holly	*Illex Aquifolium*
Hydrangea	
Lantana	*Lantana Camara*
Larkspurs	*Delphinium Species*
Lillies — Easter Lilly, Hyacinth, tulip, Camass Lily, Death Camass	*Liliaceae*
Lily of the Valley	*Convallaria Majalis*
Lupine	
Monkshood (Buttercup, Leopard Bane)	*Aconitum Napellus*
Mountain Laurel	*Kalmia Latifolia*
Narcissus (Daffodil and Jonquil)	*Narcissus Poeticus Jonquilla*
Oleander	*Nerium Oleander*
Pasque Flower	*Anemone Patens*
Poinciana	
Poinsetta	*Euphorbia Poinsettia*
Poppy	*Papaver Somniferum*
Privet	*Ligustrum Vulgare*
Rhododendron	*Rhododendron*
Snow-on-the-Mountain	*Euphorbia Marginata*
Star of Bethlehem	*Ornithogalum Umbellatum*
Trumpet Vine	*Datura*
Wisteria	*Wisteria Floribunda*
Yew (Ground Hemlock)	*Taxus Baccatta*

CHAPTER SIX

GROOMING YOUR LLAMA

Grooming is important to a llama's well-being; it helps desensitize him as well as to keep his coat shining and healthy. As you work in close proximity with the llama, he becomes familiar with your touch, his fears are eliminated and a bond will form between you. He will be more manageable and you will be attuned to his movements and moods. Different personalities will come into play; one llama will come running when you turn on the blower while another will high-tail it to the farthest reaches of the pasture.

BLOWING

Either a leaf-blower or a *Circuiteer*™ hot air blower may be used in the initial phase of grooming; be sure to follow the procedures discussed in Chapter Nine to introduce your llama to this new contraption. It may take a few days before you can actually apply air to the coat. The blower removes debris from the llama's coat and fluffs it up for better brushing. Don't hold the nozzle too close to the wool or the rotary action of the air will cause it to twirl and twist. A distance of about twelve inches will do a good job. Depending on how much foreign matter he has in his coat, it will take at least half an hour to blow an average llama. Start at the neck area, away from face or ears, and work your way along his body.

BRUSHING

Brushing is the next step, and a real job. Use a pin brush like those used in dog grooming; avoid stiff bristles or metal combs, as the llama

Using a blower can remove debris, fluff up the coat,
and help to desentitize.

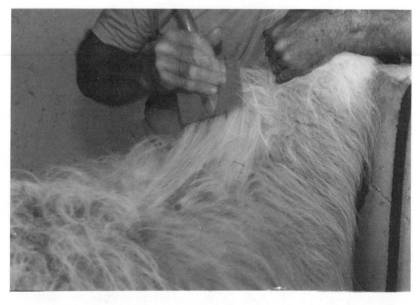

By brushing the wool back you can get to the debris underneath.
The base of the neck seems to accumulate the most straw and hay.

does not like to have his wool pulled. A boar bristle or nylon human hair brush can also be used.

Begin at the neck and work down to the back, using long gentle strokes. Talk to your llama throughout this process; this helps to distract him. Do not resort to quick jabs or tug at those mats. And don't let your llama get in the habit of moving around to avoid the brush; if he moves away from you, cross-tie or pen him in a corner.

After you have worked your way down the top-line to the tail, brush the llama's sides. Stand on one side and lean over his back to brush the side opposite you. Use your left arm and hand to sweep the wool upward from the stomach to the back, and use your right hand to brush the coat downward. Depending on the strength of your back, you may only be able to do one section at a time. Monthly brushing will maintain the coat in good condition.

SHAMPOOING

It is not generally necessary to shampoo a llama, as blowing and brushing will keep his coat healthy and clean. However, if you plan to show your llama in either halter or performance classes, you will want to bathe him for a more finished look. If you do shampoo, use a good quality, gentle product. We buy our shampoo from the local dog groomer and have been very happy with a product called *Blue Diamond®*. This shampoo particularly enhances the coat of white llamas, bleaching out any "yellows."

Pick a warm, sunny day and plan to spend about four hours to do a thorough job. Begin your project early enough in the day for your llama to be completely dry before evening. We use warm water for shampooing and rinsing, hooking our hose up to the hot water heater. If it's an extremely hot day, you can use cool (not cold) water.

First blow out the debris and brush out as many burrs as possible. Then completely soak the llama down and prepare yourself for a shock. You will realize how thin his neck really is, and how much of him is wool. This is a good time to see if he is putting on too much weight.

Apply the shampoo and dig in! Massage the wool as you would your own hair, paying particular attention to the knees and other hard-to-clean areas such as the stifle, hocks and elbows. You will be surprised to realize that you're working very close to the llama's back legs and that he doesn't seem to mind! You're desensitizing him well. A word of caution; don't use shampoo around the eyes or the ears,

Work shampoo thoroughly into the wool.

Be sure you rinse the soap completely out.

as it can badly irritate them. A damp cloth can do a very good job in these areas and isn't stressful.

After the llama is well-lathered, rinse twice, being sure to remove all of the soap. If his coat is heavily matted, a creme rinse will help remove persistent burrs. However, creme rinses sometimes weigh the wool down and leave the coat flat and limp. Rinse it out well, for the less material left on the wool, the better.

When you're ready to dry the llama, again keep the blower's nozzle far enough away from his body to avoid twisting the wool. It helps to brush while you dry; burrs and other chaff will continue to blow out.

The drying process can take several hours; if your llama gets edgy, take a few breaks and take him for a walk. Don't turn him loose, or I can guarantee that he will head for the nearest dust bowl to roll! When your task is complete, you'll be rewarded with a beautiful fluff ball that's a pleasure to handle and to show.

TRIMMING THE NAILS

When a llama is inactive or on irrigated pasture, his nails rapidly become overgrown. They should be trimmed regularly. Long, twisted nails result in lameness and affect your llama's gait and posture. Once a toenail is severely distorted, it may be impossible to correct.

You'll need a pair of farrier's short handled nippers and a pair of strong clippers that resemble big scissors (some breeders use aviation snips). Both items can be purchased at feed stores or tack shops or hardware stores. Use the nippers to snip off the hook or tip of the nail, and use the clippers to trim excess tailing along the nail's edge. If the nails are extremely long, you may need to use the nippers for the whole job. If you haven't trimmed your llama before, have someone help you. You may want your veterinarian to demonstrate the technique.

Fold the leg back so that the bottom of the foot faces upward. Then trim the toenail from the pad toward the tip. Like dogs and cats, the llama has a "quick," or vein, in its toenail; if you cut too deep, he will feel it. However, don't be concerned with minor bleeding; it's more important to remove the excess nail. If the toenail bleeds excessively, apply an antiseptic, such as Betadine wash, and keep the llama in a clean area.

If the nail has twisted, use a file to wear down the top line of the nail. This weakens the shell of the nail and permits straight new growth. Remember that overgrown nails can cause splayed toes and even a bow-legged gait.

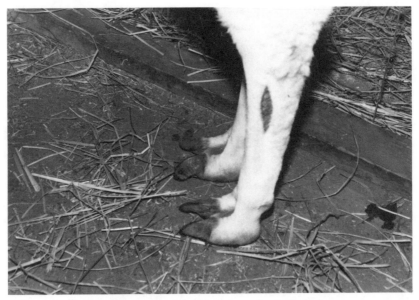

Long, misshaped nails in need of trimming.

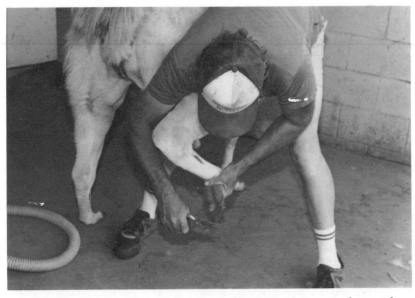

Try to get a firm hold on the rear leg. Your knee can be used
as a support.

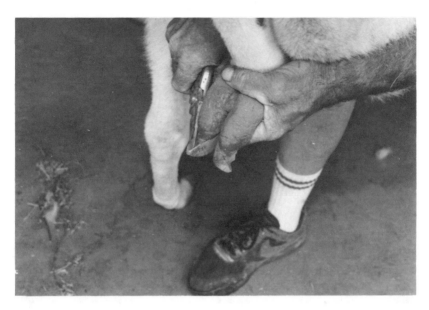

Pick out the dirt embedded in the nail and trim the sides of the nail.

Finally, snip off the tip.

Normal llama toes with correctly trimmed nails.

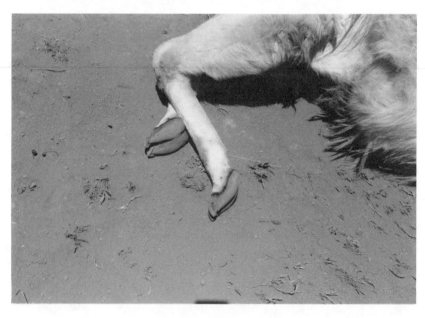

The pad on a llama's feet provide traction on steep trails and
are unique to camelids.

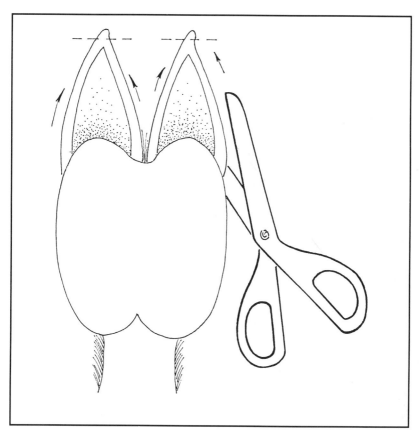

Cut the nails along each side as shown, then snip off the tip. Cut in the direction indicated.

THE FIGHTING TEETH

Both male and female llamas develop "fighting teeth" around the age of two-and-a-half years. The female's teeth are not as long as the males, and we usually aren't concerned with them. In males these teeth are double-edged and very sharp. Males in play can slash ears, bite legs and even castrate another male, so the fighting teeth need to be removed.

When I'm grooming my male llamas, I inspect their mouths to see if their teeth have erupted or if older teeth that might have been cut off earlier have grown back. Time can pass quickly and the teeth erupt before you realize it.

Veterinarians and breeders use varying techniques to remove these teeth. Since this isn't an easy job, a restraint chute is required. This procedure is painful for the llama, and often requires anesthesia.

Some breeders remove their llamas' fighting teeth by sawing off a tooth at gum-line with the use of obstetrical wire. Another technique is to make an incision below the gum line, cut the tooth below and suture the gum. Since there are fighting teeth in both upper and lower jaws, this is extensive surgery.

SHEARING

Shearing llamas is age-old in South America, but relatively new in the United States. Since the length and fullness of their llama's coat is highly important to breeders, most are hesitant to shear. Long wool is especially desirable on the herd sire; if your male llama is standing to outside females, the prospective dam's owners will want to see the length and quality of his coat. If you plan to exhibit your llama, you'll naturally want to leave his coat intact, as it takes approximately two years for a shorn coat to grow out.

Lack of knowledge about the best way to shear a llama has contributed to the slow growth of this aspect of llama ranching. When sheep are shorn, they are turned over on their backs and become almost catatonic, permitting electric shears nearly anywhere on their bodies. This is not the case with llamas — they panic. The result is flailing legs, vocalizing and "green" (spit-upon) shirts. Additionally, breeders have hesitated to stress their "ladies in waiting" by trying to shear them.

Today the trend is changing. Heat stress and obesity have negatively affected our llamas; recent research has indicated that shorn animals do better in hot weather. And when overweight llamas get rid of their heavy coats, they have more energy, exercise more, and "voila!" — they lose weight. Consequently, more breeders are learning how to shear their animals and taking on this task.

The Best Time to Shear

When to shear greatly depends on where you live. As we live in the Sierra Nevada foothills, we prefer spring. It isn't wise to shear pregnant llamas early or late in their term. Better timing is right after birthing or before breeding. They will incur less stress and less risk

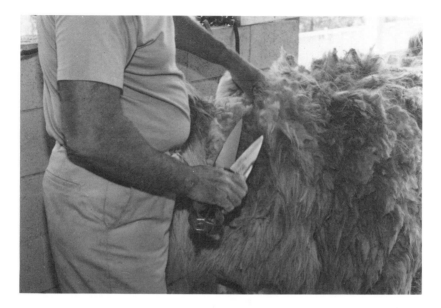

Start shearing the top line at the base of the neck.

A sheared llama will weather the summer heat better than one
in full coat.

of abortion or premature delivery. You can shear your males at almost any time of the year unless your winters are severe; then late spring is preferable.

How To Shear

Some llama ranchers tranquilize their animals for shearing, while others elect to tie them. Since anesthesia is always risky, most breeders will not use it. When using a sedative, you must be very cautious with the dosage. The amount given is based on the animal's weight, and an overdose can be lethal.

Since we keep our llamas in training to insure their manageability, we try to use shearing as a form of desensitizing. We don't use sedatives, nor do we stress an animal any longer than we have to. If I feel the tension is getting to be too much, I stop, and resume the project on another day. It's common around our ranch in spring to see llamas with half a coat! I use a large scissors designed for this purpose, as electric clippers can cut too close to the skin if you're not extremely careful.

Leave approximately two inches of the coat; llamas sunburn and may sustain shock if left with no coat. Using shears, you can take your time and easily leave the protective length. You'll need an assistant, for llamas hate haircuts and consider removal of their wool to be assault with a deadly weapon!

Cross-tie the llama and try to box him into a corner. Your assistant should reassure him, standing at his head. Leave the neck wool intact, as it is normally shorter and hard to spin and weave. Clip the wool along the top-line, working from the base of the neck and ending at the base of the tail. Leave the tail intact for fly control and communication.

After you take off the top wool, work down each side from high on the back to low on the side. Move to the chest, and then the haunches. Remove all the wool around the back of the rump. The llama's "thermal windows", which allow heating and cooling of the body from external sources, are his legs, stomach and rear thighs. By removing the excess fiber, you are allowing the air to flow in this area, thus cooling your llama. Shearing adult females removes long strands of wool that might wrap around the penis during breeding. The tip of the penis can actually be cut if caught in tight wool.

After shearing, llamas may feel ostracized by or embarrassed in front of the rest of the herd. Some hide in the barn and will not come out. Thus, when you've sheared your llama, put him alone in a stall or corral and give him time to recover his dignity. When you've finished the second animal, you can put the two together. Additionally, give your llama time to acclimate to the weather; don't put him directly outside in bright sunlight on a hot day.

El Cid, one of our males, pretends he is king of the ranch. Last spring when I had finished shearing our females and still had some energy, I noticed that he was starting to look very shaggy. I thought that a little trim here and there might improve his appearance. He disagreed, but I snipped away. The more I cut, the more he drooped. I continually reassured him that he was beautiful and gave him loving pats, but he stood stock-still with a resigned look that said, "Just get it over with."

When he was shorn of all the heavy mats I opened the door to our outer corral. He cautiously approached the opening and peeked outside. The other two breeding males in adjoining corrals were curiously waiting for him to emerge. It was like watching teenagers preparing to harass their peers. El Cid took one look, snorted loudly, and returned to a far corner of the stall. Nothing I did could make him go outside. It was three days before he finally ventured out, and then with far less bravado. However, within a week he was himself again, strutting around the pasture cooler and happier.

MARKETING THE WOOL

At every exhibit and county fair people ask me about the possibility of buying wool. Llama owners often overlook the value of their animals' wool; it is distinctly different from other fibers, and highly valued by wool spinners. It doesn't have the oiliness or the lanolin content of sheep's wool and is extremely soft. However, it is often shorter and harder to spin. Some spinners mix llama and sheep wool to achieve a more manageable combination. Most major mills want the wool to be four or more inches long so that it can be machine-spun more easily.

The current price for llama wool ranges from $2 to $5 per ounce depending on the quality, cleanliness, and length of fiber. The amount of crimp in the fiber, which aids in the adhering of individual strands to one another, is also important. Clean the wool as much as possible by picking out debris, straw, alfalfa and burrs. Separate the colors as much as you can.

The best wool is accumulated when shampooing and drying your llama. During the show season when we groom heavily we constantly fill the wool bags in our barn. This wool sells for about $4 per ounce.

If you don't find private wool buyers, approach members of the weavers' guild in your area, or attend county fairs and ask the artisans there if they would be interested. Although wool sales can supplement your income, you'll be surprised by how much it takes to make a pound; don't plan to make the house payment with it! You may find great reward in growing, carding, and spinning wool, and knitting or weaving your own garments, scarves and hats.

CHAPTER SEVEN

PREVENTATIVE HEALTH CARE

In order to properly care for your llamas and start off on the right foot with a health maintenance program, you need to know the basics of veterinary care. The data within these pages should be used only as a general guideline to help you assess what to do yourself and how to do it, versus when to call your veterinarian. When in doubt consult an expert.

Some llama owners are happy with their veterinarian, but realize that he or she is not comfortable treating their unusual animal. Discuss this with your veterinarian and see if he would be willing to have you sponsor him at some of the llama expos or attend veterinary panels at seminars. He will then be able to pair his own background with the latest developments in the industry and can save the time and expense of traveling long distances for help elsewhere.

In addition to the insight your veterinarian gains from symposiums, he may avail himself of The International Llama Association's medical hotline; make sure he has this number, if you join the Association.

VITAL STATISTICS

The adult llama's normal body temperature ranges from 99.5 – 101.5 F (or 37.5 – 38.6 C). Neonate (newborn) temperatures have a slightly greater range of 99.0 – 102.0 F or (37.2 – 38.9 C.) Temperature can elevate one to two degrees or more if the weather is warm and/or the llama has been very active.

Any type of rectal thermometer can be used to determine temperature. You can buy a livestock thermometer at your feed or vet supply store. We prefer the digital variety, as it is faster to read and less apt to break. Some breeders attach a string with a clothespin to clip to the wool. If you don't have an assistant to stand at the llama's head,

A pack trip is much more enjoyable with a llama to carry your supplies. This photo of Paul Barkman by Betty Barkman, at Point Reyes, California.

halter and tie him before you begin. Shake the thermometer down before you use it, and lubricate the end with *K-Y Jelly®* or Vaseline™. Insert it into the rectum no more than two inches for three minutes.

The llama's respiration rate is 10-30 per minute or one cycle every five seconds. The pulse rate is 60-99 per minute. Neonates generally have higher pulse rates. The best way to record the pulse rate is to place a stethoscope on the left chest area under the left elbow. Count the number of beats in fifteen seconds and multiply by four to get your per minute rate.

SIGNS OF ILLNESS

Llamas are very stoic, rarely showing pain until an illness has progressed. For this reason if for no other, become familiar with the individual personalities and habits of each llama. Their movements, posture, and behavior should be closely observed so that you know what is normal. Then, when one of the llamas is sick, the owner will KNOW that something is wrong. The call to the veterinarian might begin with, "I can't put my finger on anything, but he just isn't acting right.

. . . " Don't overlook strange behavior, it may be the only signal you will get.

Other symptoms to watch for include a discharge from the eyes, nose, mouth, vagina; change in the stool; weight loss; limping or stiffness; difficult breathing; difficulty in urinating or defecating; growths or lumps; or irregular or noisy breathing.

PARASITES

Parasite prevention is part of all livestock management, and llamas are no exception. Routine fecal exams, removal of dung, and pasture rotation are all important measures.

Many llama owners routinely worm the whole herd, while others feel that it is better to perform fecal flotations to check for parasites before having a llama ingest unnecessary chemicals. Place a few pellets of dung in a plastic baggie, label with each animal's name, and deliver promptly to your vet. Or buy a microscope kit and have your veterinarian teach you to do your own fecals.

A good preventative measure if you have the room is pasture rotation. This gives the grass a chance to recuperate and grow, but more importantly, the llamas are not as apt to eat the grass so far down that they pick up worm eggs. If you don't have extra space, make it a practice to haul or blade dung out of your pastures.

Internal Parasites

Liver Flukes — Fascioliasis — better known as liver flukes, affect the liver of the llama. Found in the temperate and tropical zones, liver flukes need snail hosts to complete their life cycles. If you contain your llamas near marshy, swamplike areas, be alert to the potential for this infection. The symptoms of liver flukes include weight loss and depression. Affected llamas become anemic and anorexic.

Fluke eggs are difficult to detect on fecal flotation. If your llama is affected, follow your veterinarian's recommendation for treatment.

Coccidia eimeria — These parasites are found in all species of animals. The tiny protozoa take up residence in the intestines where they cause weight loss and diarrhea. Coccidiosis is very common in llamas in North America and is very serious in South America.

Tapeworms — The incidence of tapeworms is increasing, possibly because ordinary worming procedures do not attack and kill this parasite. The llama may show weight loss, may go off feed, and occasionally

Paste worming is easy. First, locate the space between the teeth.

Then inject the measured amount
of paste with a push of the plunger.

have diarrhea. For most breeders, the first indication of tapeworms
may be the appearance of white segments in the stool. Treatment is
difficult, and you should consult your veterinarian.

Meningeal Worm — Meningeal worms are a problem in the eastern
United States. With the increase in transportation of llamas from coast
to coast, the problem is spreading. White-tailed deer act as a host in
the life cycle of the meningeal worm. If you are in an area inhabited
by the white-tail, learn more about this parasite from your veterinarian.

Symptoms of meningeal worm infection include weakness, stagger-
ing and paralysis. Once signs develop, prognosis is poor; to date, the
best prevention is to keep white-tail deer out of your pastures.

Other stomach and intestinal worms that infest llamas include the
thread-necked Strongyle, Nodular, Whip Worm, and Tread Worm.
Most llamas will be host to some or all of these parasites. Treatment
should be under the supervision of your veterinarian. Wormers are
generally administered as needed or in the spring and fall on a routine
basis.

Eperythrozoonosis (EPE) — In early 1989, various veterinary teaching schools began to see cases of EPE. The llamas were extremely
anemic. EPE is a red blood cell protozoan parasite found in various
mammalian species. This particular parasite can create illness on its
own or debilitate an animal that is already suffering from pneumonia,

ulcers or infection. It appears to attack only a system that is already low in immunity. At this time, it is too early to make conclusions as to the cause, diagnosis and treatment. It is recommended that llama owners and their veterinarians keep abreast of ongoing developments in this area.

External Parasites

Sarcoptic mange — The mange mite burrows into the skin of its victims, causing severe coat loss. The skin becomes thickened and scaly. There will be hair loss and scabs in the affected areas. To detect these mites, a skin scraping must be examined under a microscope. Early detection is extremely important, as a whole herd can become infected. Check with your veterinarian for treatment. In the past, *Ivermectin* injections have been the most successful, and we seldom see sarcoptic mange today.

Lice and Fleas — Lice come in biting and sucking varieties. Sucking lice are more debilitating, affect the wool quality and cause the llama to become anemic. Llamas infested with lice constantly scratch and rub along fence posts and walls. You can see louse eggs, or nits, when examining wool strands. Louse powder can be very effective; however, it has to be re-applied in ten to fourteen days to kill eggs that have hatched after initial treatment.

Fleas also affect llamas, causing continuous scratching and rubbing. They can become infected from exposure to other animals or areas infested with fleas. Treatment is the same as for lice. Bedding and barn areas should also be treated to avoid reinfestation.

Flies — These common everyday pests create more owner headaches than anything else. Llamas will shake their heads and rub their faces in the grass to escape. Flies lay their eggs (maggots) in dung piles, the corners of eyes, and in open wounds. Besides being a nuisance, some species cause pain.

Breeders use various deterrents including fly-paper and actual fly-traps. Frequent clean-up of dung piles and stabling areas is the best prevention. Parasitic wasps constitute a recent innovation; these tiny creatures about the size of ants, will not bite either humans or llamas and they can be ordered from farm supply houses, and deposited around dung piles. The adult wasps lay eggs on fly larvae and prevent them from hatching.

Bot flies deposit eggs in the llama's nasal cavities. Bots cause a runny nose and head-shaking. Consult your veterinarian.

Ticks — Found all over North America, ticks are both soft and hard-bodied. Hard-bodied ticks are prevalent in western areas of the country. On a minor scale, they infest the llamas ears, causing him to shake his head constantly; often, one ear will hang at a 90° angle. To troubleshoot this problem, halter and secure the llama. Look down the ear canal with a flashlight to see if the problem is a tick or a foxtail. The ear canal is very deep, making it difficult to observe the unwanted tenants. Just because you don't see them, doesn't mean they aren't there. NEVER stick foreign objects down the ear canal. Your veterinarian has the instruments necessary. If ticks are the culprits, they can be easily treated by dousing the ear canal with a mixture of *Permectrin®* and mineral oil. During heavy tick infestation, we routinely douse the ears as a preventative measure.

At the other end of the spectrum, some ticks can cause paralysis. However, the problem is FINDING the tick. You may have to resort to shearing the animal. When the tick is found, its whole body, including the head, must be carefully removed with a tweezers.

Ticks also carry other diseases, including Lyme disease, a growing health threat that is spread by ticks from wildlife to livestock, pets and people. The best tick prevention is routine spraying of the llamas. Your veterinarian can inform you as to types of sprays available and frequency of application in your area.

FOXTAIL

Besides the poisonous plants mentioned in Chapter 5, there is another plant that can cause considerable harm. The foxtail is aptly named since the awn or seed bearing tip of the plant does resemble a fox's tail. In the summer months when the plant has dried out, the foxtails scatter throughout pastures.

When the awn secures itself in the fleece of the llama, or the fur of a dog or cat, it starts to work its way into the skin. The foxtail can penetrate the epidermis, muscle and even bone. One llama has been known to die from a foxtail that entered the ear and ended up in the brain. Since the foxtail can easily penetrate thin-skinned and moist areas, the ears, eyes, mouth and nostrils are the most likely spots to be affected by these culprits. A foxtail can work itself deep down inside an eyelid. In an attempt to escape the pain of the invader, the llama will rub his eye on fenceposts and walls of the barn, sometimes scratching and scarring the cornea. Whenever you see swollen eyes, be immediately suspicious of a foxtail and contact your veterinarian. The animal may have to be sedated to facilitate removal.

DIGESTIVE DISORDERS

Choking

Choking can be a frightening experience. Greedy animals will bolt their food without chewing, and large chunks of apples or carrots can become lodged in the esophagus. This situation is not uncommon in llamas. The llama will extend its neck, cough, shake its head, retch and seem very alarmed.

First try to calm the llama, then palpate the throat to find the obstruction. Gently flush the mouth with water, and if the obstruction does not clear, it's time to call the veterinarian. He may have to use a stomach tube to push the object down. DO NOT stick your hand into the llama's mouth. Llamas have sharp teeth and may bite in panic.

Make it a habit to patrol your pastures, picking up foreign objects that a curious llama might nibble. Cut carrots and apples into small pieces and control the hasty eater who gobbles his grain or pellets by placing large rocks in the feeder so that they have to eat around them.

Colic

Colic in llamas is very similar to that seen in horses, and as with these animals, most of the time a cause is difficult if not impossible to detect. Sometimes the condition may be linked to overeating grain, ingesting poisonous plants or mildewed hay or having a feast in the apple orchard.

The symptoms of colic are often subtle and may include a lack of appetite, laying with hind legs out to the side instead of kushed, bloating of the stomach, grinding of teeth, kicking at the belly, constant restlessness, getting up and down, rolling, and strange, unusual stances. The animal is obviously in pain. If you have ever had an attack of gastritis, you can imagine what a llama in colic is going through.

Mineral oil is sometimes the best treatment, with an analgesic to dull the pain. Your veterinarian can give the dosages and recommend a pain killer.

Gastric Ulcers

Gastric ulcers can exist in a llama without any overt symptoms. The most obvious signs will be lack of appetite and isolating from the herd. Unfortunately, we are not certain of either causes or treatment for ulcers. We suspect that llamas, similar to humans, develop ulcers as a result of extreme stress and an overly rich diet. Ulcers can perforate and bleed. Watch the lone llama that avoids the dinner table, and consult your veterinarian.

Impaction

Impaction is caused when the stool is prolonged in the gut and dehydrated by decreased water intake. The llama will urinate but not defecate. He will be extremely listless, and spend most of the time in the sitting position. Impaction is a common cause of colic. Early detection and prompt veterinary treatment are the keys to recovery.

Torsion

Torsion is a condition where the intestines and colon become twisted, also causing impaction and eventual death. Symptoms are similar to colic. Immediate veterinary treatment and possibly surgery are required.

INFECTIOUS DISEASES

Vaccination Schedule

Llamas are subject to a number of infectious diseases as are other domesticated animals. Some will be common to your area; some will not. Consult with your veterinarian and set up an annual vaccination schedule. In California, we vaccinate annually with CDT. Pregnant llamas are given a booster thirty to forty-five days prior to parturition. Crias receive their first shots at eight weeks and a second series at twelve weeks, and thereafter on an annual schedule. Additional vaccines such as 5-way leptospirosis, rabies and equine rhinopneumonitis may be recommended by your veterinarian.

Tetanus

Tetanus, also known as lockjaw, is carried by a bacteria which can survive in soil or rusty metal for years. The clostridium tetani bacteria that causes this disease is commonly found in the ground around stables, buildings and areas previously occupied by horses and cattle. The bacteria enters the body through wounds, especially those of a puncture type. Since this bacteria prefers anaerobic (low oxygen) areas, deep cuts or punctures give the most ideal conditions for it's growth.

Symptoms include a saw-horse stance, rigid muscles, a fixed stare and a clamped mouth (hence the term lockjaw). The disease is often fatal.

All llamas should be boostered annually with tetanus toxoid.

Blackleg

Blackleg is a disease of ruminants that is often seen in this country. Check with your veterinarian for problems in your area.

Enterotoxemia

Clostridium Perfringens is another bacteria that dislikes oxygen. It is found in the gastro-intestinal tract of the llama; even healthy llamas can carry it. Problems develop when other conditions break down the healthy environment in the intestines. Then the organisms grow and create toxins that are harmful to the host. Five types of enterotoxemia are known: A,B,C,D, & E. Llamas are susceptible to types A, C and possibly D. Symptoms can be varied and even contradictory. Diarrhea, constipation, marked high and low temperatures and movements similar to colic. The abdomen is usually extended and the cria will stretch the head forward, eyes closed, with the ears back in a reclined position. Death can ensue within hours.

This disease occurs most often in crias; therefore, it is very important to inoculate the dam prior to birthing. Other preventative measures include good sanitary practices on the ranch.

Leptospirosis

A few cases of leptospirosis have been reported in llamas. It is caused by a microorganism that produces the disease in all mammals, including man. Rodents are a reservoir for infection though water contamination. The organisms attack the kidneys, liver, and reproductive systems. Infected urine is passed into ponds where it will infect any animal drinking from that same source. Symptoms include fever, anemia, pulmonary congestion and abortion. Vaccines are available to protect against this disease. Your veterinarian will know which vaccines are needed in your area.

Rabies

Rabies is a viral disease transmitted in the saliva of infected animals. Symptoms of the disease include jerking the head, running wildly, trembling, irritability and attacking other animals and people. Any bite from an animal should be suspect. The wound should be cleansed and the victim isolated and watched closely. If possible, try to isolate the animal that inflicted the wound so that it can be observed for the disease.

Any warm-blooded animal can carry rabies; however if you live in an area where there are bats, raccoons and skunks, you should have your llama vaccinated. The vaccine used MUST be the killed variety.

Foot and Mouth Disease

This is a highly contagious disease and outbreaks of FMD can be devastating to all livestock. There was on outbreak in Canada in 1952 that cost that country 130 million dollars. The United States had outbreaks in 1902, 1908, 1914-15 and 1924-25. Complete herds of cattle, swine and sheep had to be destroyed, disinfected, and buried.

Currently there is no Foot and Mouth Disease in North America. However, as more and more llamas and alpacas are being imported into the United States, and if the quarantine requirements become less stringent and restrictive, the chance of another outbreak is possible. Chile has been relatively free of the disease, but Bolivia and Peru have had reported cases. The borders between these countries are not rigidly patrolled and smugglers can easily transport animals from one country to another.

The virus may be harbored in the pharynx of the carrier and in some species may live there for over two years without any clinical signs of the disease. Lesions occur on the lips, tongues, nostrils and on the feet. Early signs are fever and anorexia. FMD is fatal and at the present time there is no treatment. All suspected cases must be reported to state and federal authorities for quarantine and diagnosis. Under the law, infected animals and all those exposed to the disease must be euthanized.

Tuberculosis

Tuberculosis is a bacterial infectious disease in which tubercles or nodules form on various organs of the body. Llamas are not highly

Llasa's Princess Daisy at nine months old just after winning Reserve Grand Champion at the 1988 Sonoma-Marin Llama Extravaganza.

susceptible to tuberculosis, but a few cases have been reported. The clinical signs of this disease are emaciation and weight loss. Treatment is not allowed in the United States and vaccines are illegal, so affected animals are destroyed.

Brucellosis

Brucellosis causes abortion during the last trimester of pregnancy. Not considered a major disease in llamas, it is found predominantly in cattle, sheep and goats. However, many states require that llamas be tested for brucellosis before crossing state lines.

CHAPTER EIGHT

FIRST AID

Accidents happen to every livestock owner. Most will be minor, but it pays to be prepared. We keep the phone number of our veterinarian readily accessible both in the home and in the barn. Also close at hand is the medical box.

VETERINARY SUPPLIES

There are certain items that every llama owner should have on hand for medical emergencies and everyday care. We use the kind of box sold in stationery stores for storing files; the lift-up lid makes it easy to survey the contents quickly and to keep out dirt and dust. The box should be stored in a clean, dry area of the barn and be readily accessible.

Since most emergencies tend to happen either at night or on the weekends when the stores are closed, purchase your supplies ahead of time.

Recommended Inventory

Needles: 20 gauge x 1"; 19 gauge x 1"
Syringes: 3cc; 12cc; 35cc dose; 60cc dose; turkey baster — ear syringe
BIOHAZARD CONTAINER!
Injectables — with veterinarian's approval:
    Torbutrol
    Dyprone
    Banamine "?" Situational — possibly on the trail
    Steroids "?" Situational
Orals: Butazolidin paste or tablets; activated charcoal
Ointments, Sprays:
    Ophthalmic antibiotic
    Ophthalmic rinse — Visine, Murine

Topical antibiotic — Furacin, Bacitracin, betadine, Furox spray
Tinactin
Vaseline Jelly
KY Jelly
Solutions/Suspensions: Hydrogen peroxide; 7% iodine; betadine;
Coppertox — Blue stone; mineral oil; Pepto Bismol; Clorox
Insecticides: Fly repellants — ointments, sprays; Permectrin — ears
Wormers: Invermectin paste — injectable; Panacur; etc.
Miscellaneous: Fleet enemas 4 oz — give one-half
Wrap Materials: Telfa pads; moleskin; Vetwrap — Coban; Elasticon —
Conform — 2"; duct tape
Equipment:
Stomach tubes — Red rubber 18/20 french
Enema tube/can
Hoof trimmers
Mouth speculum — PVC pipe
Hemostat
Suture material — fishing line — nonabsorbable material
Rectal thermometers — one to use, one to drop
Urine cup — pole — baby food jar
Film container — shot glass
Tweezers — for foxtails
Electric clippers
Hair curlers
Scissors
OB gloves/disposable gloves
For the Trail: Socks, boots, "man-packed" panniers
Might Be Nice: Stethoscope
Forget: Otoscope; alligator forceps

Some of these items are for plant poisoning, and you should check
with your veterinarian on the dosage by weight for llamas, as opposed
to those for horses and cows. Keep a record of these amounts in the
first aid kit.

RESTRAINT AND HANDLING

In any emergency situation, it is important that you don't panic.
Talk softly to the llama, reassuring him, but be firm in your handling.
If a llama feels that he has a chance to escape, he will try. Try to calm
his fears and give him confidence that you are going to help him.

In the event that your llama is not trained to stand quietly, you may have to use some restraint techniques. Always halter the llama and keep a firm hand on the lead rope. If a wooden (not wire) fence or solid wall is available, position the llama next to it to help confine him. If a stock restrainer or chute is not available, you can use a horse trailer or small stall.

Another form of restraint is to reach over the side of the llama, placing some of your body weight on his back. With both hands, grab a handful of fleece, one hand behind the elbow and the other toward the lower back side of the llama.

Or you can stand at the llama's withers, lean over the back with your right hand and grab a handful of fleece on the right shoulder region. Then grab a handful of fleece with the left hand near the shoulder next to you. Apply your body weight to the back. The llama should stand quietly.

There are several llama restraint chutes on the market and if you are contemplating purchasing one, spend some time investigating the features of each; llamas have been known to be injured by the stocks themselves. We prefer "The Llama Work Station" (see appendix).

When tying a llama, quick release safety snaps are important to insure you can release the animal quickly if necessary.

The practice of "earing" is not commonly used unless there is an emergency. If you have to resort to earing, use the following procedure. Stand to the left side next to the withers and extend your right arm over the back and up the neck. Gradually slide your hand up the neck and firmly grasp the base of the ear with your whole hand. Be careful that the llama doesn't butt his head against your face while trying to avoid your hand. Squeeze firmly until the llama "freezes." You may need to squeeze the left ear with your left hand also.

Restraint of Neonates

Crias are far easier to handle, chiefly because of their size. The correct way to carry a young llama is to place one arm around the chest while the other arm is extended under the llama forward of the rear legs, but behind the stomach.

Another way to restrain a cria is to have him in a position where he is kushed with all the legs tucked underneath. The handler then assumes a kneeling position that straddles the little one. This is the same position that we use while bottle feeding. Be sure not to sit back on the llama, as your weight could do damage to his spine. This method is particularly effective when taking his temperature, or checking the head, sucking reflexes, and teeth.

If your cria has not been halter-trained, the time for treatment is not the time to put on the first halter. He will be fighting you as well as the halter and could injure his neck. The memory of the experience could make him difficult to halter for the rest of his life.

TREATMENT OF COMMON INJURIES

Cuts

Cuts can come from thousands of items: fence wire, sharp rocks, irrigating equipment, or the fighting teeth of other llamas to name a few. Secure the llama before examining and treating. If the wound is bleeding excessively, direct pressure with a towel or cloth is the best way to stop the flow. Spurting blood signifies that an artery has been affected and you need to call your veterinarian immediately. Keep pressure on the injury until help arrives.

Some cuts can be handled at home and do not require stitches. Always clean your hands before cleansing the wound. *Betadine®* diluted with water makes a good scrub. Use clean sterile gauze pads soaked in *Betadine®* to gently remove any foreign debris. Flushing the cut can be done with a large syringe with the needle removed or by using a plastic bottle with a pointed tip available at your pharmacist. Fill the syringe with clean water, or water that has been diluted with *Betadine®* to the color of sun tea. Douse the interior of the cut until there are no visible signs of debris.

For added protection, lightly cover the injured area with water soluble *Neosporin®* ointment and apply a sterile pad. The pad can be held in place with adhesive tape or veterinary wrap. If the cut is on the foot pad, we secure the covering with duct tape since it is stronger and holds up better with wear.

The dressing should be changed daily and removed when the cut has closed. If the wound is very deep, check to see if the llama's tetanus shots are current. If not, administer a tetanus booster.

Cuts to the Ear

On occasion, fighting teeth on the males can erupt before you are aware of it, two males will have a spat, and all of a sudden you have a torn ear. Males in play will always go for the ears and testicles. Rinse the ear cut with clear water and make arrangements with your veterinarian to have it stitched within a few hours. Once the blood clots and the healing process begins it will be more difficult to repair the damage. The ear has a lot of cartilage and little excess skin to reattach. Do not apply hydrogen peroxide or iodine as both of these have a cauterizing effect, thus sealing the edges of the skin.

Cuts to the Testicles
If your llama has had severe bites on the testicle, cleanse the area as you would for any of the above and have your veterinarian immediately assess the damage. It would be a financial loss to have your future herd sire accidentally gelded by a playful partner when the situation may be corrected.

Electrical Shock
The most important thing to do in the case of electrical shock is to TURN OFF THE POWER. If the source of the electrical current is a tank heater, be careful not to come in contact with the water in or around the tank. Do not attempt to move the llama or any wires until the power is off. You could be electrocuted also. After the source of the problem has been eliminated, then turn to the victim. If the llama is not breathing, begin artificial respiration. Place the llama on his right side (this puts less pressure on the heart). Do not allow a llama to lie on his back with his feet in the air. In this position, the contents of the stomach can be aspirated into the lungs. Roll him on his right side, or if you have a helper, try to prop him into a kushing position.

Artificial Respiration
If the llama is not breathing, kneel by his shoulder. Slide both hands down the llama's side until you reach the last rib. Grab the rib and lift up and back towards the shoulder. When the lungs are expanded, release the rib and push down on the ribs closest to the shoulder. Repeat this exercise every five seconds and keep it up until the llama is breathing or help comes.

When some animals "come to" they will dash wildly around the paddock. Prepare for this sudden burst of energy and restrain the llama.

Broken Bones
If you suspect or know that your llama has a broken bone, the first thing to do is to get the animal into a quiet stall or restrain him where he cannot do more harm to himself. Reassure him and keep him calm. Call the veterinarian immediately and unless you are experienced with emergency splinting, leave the animal alone. Trying to put a splint on a llama while he is struggling could do additional harm to

Photo by Betty Barkman.

the tips of the broken bones. The veterinarian can sedate the llama before proceeding.

Shock

If a llama has been severely traumatized in an injury or accident, shock can set in. Every mechanism within the system goes "on hold," and slows down. Signs of shock are irregular breathing, a reduced pulse rate and pale gums and eyelids.

Check the airways to make sure they are clear. Try to place the llama in a kushed position and keep him warm if the weather is cold. Avoid over-warming; usually a blanket over the stomach and legs is sufficient. Call your veterinarian.

Poisoning

Poisoning can result from eating poisonous plants, pesticides and chemicals. Symptoms of poisoning can vary greatly, depending on the cause. You may see any of the following: vomiting, convulsions, diarrhea, foaming at the mouth, colic, muscle twitching, weakness, difficulty breathing and an irregular heartbeat. Most important is to pinpoint the poison, so when you call the veterinarian he can prescribe the proper antidote and treatment. Prevention is the safer way to go, since there are few antidotes or specific treatments. Avoid the use of lead-based paints in the barn or on the fence posts. Llamas, especially crias, love to chew on anything. Become familiar with the poisonous plants in your area or in areas where you plan to backpack. A call to your local agricultural extension agent will help at home with plants common to your home area, while a call to the Forest Service can identify poisonous plants where you plan to trek. Beautiful shrubs found in everyday landscaping can be deadly. Some of these include varieties of the Yew, Azaleas, Rhododendrons and Oleander. Most important, at home and in the barn, keep pesticides, chemicals and the grain supply in areas that the llama cannot reach. A locked room is safest. We have llamas who can open gates.

Bites

Bites should be treated the same way as cuts and wounds. They should be cleansed carefully. If the llama has been bitten by a strange animal, take the same precautions as you would for Rabies.

Snake Bites — Snake bites are more frightening to you than to the llama. Venomous snakes in the United States and Canada are the rattlesnake, the water moccasin (cottonmouth), the copperhead and the coral snake. Copperheads are found in the eastern United States and their venom is not as deadly as the others. The coral snake's habitat is in Florida, Texas and Arizona. The coral variety prefers dark, hidden areas and are not likely found in open pastures. The water moccasin or cottonmouth inhabits the marshes and swamps of the Southeastern United States. The last remaining type of snake is the rattlesnake and is the most hazardous to the llama.

Llamas are extremely curious and will immediately investigate anything unusual. Shoving their noses into the face of a snake invites a serious bite. Llamas can be bitten on the legs as well. Any snakebite warrants a call to the veterinarian.

Although it has been suggested that you clean a bite on the leg and apply an ice pack to reduce swelling, or even apply a tourniquet above the bite, the best course of action is *to transport your llama to the veterinarian as soon as possible.*

Bites to the face can be serious, since the resulting swelling can block the air passages. Call a veterinarian immediately. If it will be some time before he can see the llama, he may want you to insert a plastic tracheal tube or a woman's hair curler so that the llama will be able to breathe. The tube must be inserted before the swelling closes the nasal passages.

There has been a great deal of debate on how to reduce snake populations. Since we live in an area of rattlesnake habitats, we were very concerned until an old timer gave me some advice. I used it and we have never seen a rattlesnake.

His remarks were to get rid of the berry bushes along the pond and creek. Snakes like to prey on the critters that eat the berries and drink from the creek. Most important was to import all the cats I could, not the fancy household type but the rangiest, hungriest and meanest ones. My response was that I didn't think cats ate snakes. His answer was, "The cats eat the mice. If there are no mice, there ain't no snakes." So off we went to the pound.

Abscesses

Abscesses are caused by injuries, usually punctures. Bacteria enters the wound and grows while the outer layer of skin closes and heals. The cavity within the injury fills with pus and swells. Whenever you see a swelling on the body, particularly the face, neck or legs, be suspicious of an abscess. Teeth can abscess, causing a lump on the outer jaw. However, some llamas will store food in the sides of the mouth, similar to a chipmunk, so make sure that this is not the situation before you call the veterinarian.

Abscesses need medical attention, since they should be lanced, irrigated and allowed to drain. Antibiotics are usually administered.

THERMAL STRESS

Heat stress

When the body temperature exceeds the high range of normal (over 103 degrees F.), your llama may be experiencing hyperthermia. This condition occurs during extremely hot days, or when a llama has been overworked on the trail during hot weather.

In the early stages, symptoms include salivating from the mouth, open-mouthed breathing, increased pulse and respiratory rate and sweating. The sweating can be detected under the chest and on the belly. As the situation gets worse, the temperature can rise to as high as 109 degrees F or more and the llama becomes uncoordinated, stands in a sawhorse position and ceases to sweat as a result of dehydration. Death may result.

A four-month-old cria. *Photo by June Cheney.*

Cool the body immediately. Provide shade with a tarp or awning. Put a fan over the llama and with a hose, let water flow over the stomach, chest and legs, or if you are on the trail lead the animal into a stream or pond and allow the water to flow over these areas. These parts of the llama body are the thermal windows. Simply dousing the llama is not enough. A constant flow of cool water over these areas is most effective. You can give a cool water enema with a turkey baster, but then it will be difficult to monitor the body temperature rectally. Crushed ice can be packed under the belly and between the legs. Results can be dramatic, however; the llama should be watched closely for a few days after the episode. Animals that have apparently recovered can die hours later from blood clots caused by the hyperthermia.

Again, prevention is the best course of action. Llamas have been known to have hyperthermia when the outside temperature was only in the 80's, so be prepared. In hot weather your llama must have access to shade as well as water. Llamas will stand in ponds, water troughs and over sprinklers. If you live in a temperate zone, investigate the overhead misters used by some breeders. Placing fans in your barn area or building sand boxes that can be soaked with water also will help.

Be particularly concerned if your llama is dark-colored (dark colors absorb the sun more), is obese or has heavy wool. We shear our wooly guys in the spring. After all, their health is more important than impressing ranch visitors. If you do shear, be sure to leave about 1½ – 2" of wool as protection from sunburn. Some breeders apply veterinarian wrap to the tail, so that air can flow around the rectal area. Avoid breeding during hot temperatures to avoid overstressing the male, and don't plan any births during the hot months. High protein grain and alfalfa should be eliminated from the diet and grass or oat hay substituted. Any stressful situations, such as training, toenail trimming, grooming or medical treatment should be reserved for the cooler morning or evening hours.

Hypothermia

Hypothermia is more common with crias than with adult llamas, especially if the newborn has been presented in an open field on a cold day or is premature. (For treatment of the newborn, refer to Chapter 12.)

Adults can usually handle cold weather unless temperatures are extreme and strong winds prevail. A high wind chill factor can reduce the temperature drastically. There is the risk of frostbite on the ears. Prevention includes shelter from the wind, rain and snow.

CHAPTER NINE

TRAINING BASICS

Llama's are intelligent and adventuresome, so training them is rewarding and not extremely difficult. We encourage new owners to educate their own companion rather than buying a pre-trained llama; it helps to build trust between owner and llama. As your llama learns each lesson, you'll have a great sense of accomplishment. You will comprehend his personality and know his limits — how far to push him in each lesson. This is generally true whether you are training a weanling cria or an adult. An older llama sometimes brings previous handling or lack thereof with him, so training him may be more challenging.

If you don't have time to train your llama, buy one that is trained or pay an expert to do it for you. Taking him on treks will build his confidence in you and he will eventually perform as well as if he had learned his abc's from you.

The llama is not born domesticated. He must be taught carefully and the trainer must be firm and patient. Whether your training goal is to halter or ground-drive your llama or teach him to pack, some general rules apply. First, be in a good frame of mind. Don't try to train your llama when you are angry or upset. Your pupil will detect your tension, and you may have a struggle on your hands!

Second, have a clear lesson plan in mind; your message must be clear and consistent.

Third, talk often to your llama and use consistent commands such as "come", "stand," and "stop." When he complies, praise and praise again. Use consistent words as positive reinforcement: "Goodboy — that's right!" He will respond to your tone of voice. Reward with a treat, like a few alfalfa pellets or a pat on his neck, when the lesson demands that the llama enter unfamiliar territory, walk over a bridge or jump into a van or trailer. Once you earn his trust, he will follow you anywhere. You might trick him once, but you won't succeed the second time! Never strike an animal or threaten with a whip or any other object. The old adage "you get more with honey than you do with vinegar" certainly applies to llama training.

If you become frustrated, impatient or angry, stop! You may be giving your llama mixed messages, pushing him too far too fast, or not praising him enough. Step back, analyze what you're doing, and patiently resume with consistent patient signals.

Fourth, end the lesson on a positive note. The llama must comply with you even if you have to abandon your original goal and settle for a lesser accomplishment. Stop when he has done what you ask and you have rewarded him.

Finally, keep the lessons short but frequent. It is optimum to work for twenty minutes to half an hour twice a day. When a llama is stressed, he'll burp, and you'll hear gurgling sounds in the throat and stomach. When you hear this, you know it's time to take a break or stop. A ruminant, the llama brings up the bolus or cud for rechewing; it is this material that he spits during a confrontation. Stressful situations confuse the llama; he doesn't appear to really want to spit at you, but is experiencing our equivalent of "heartburn."

WHEN TO TRAIN

If you've purchased a weanling male or female, or an adult llama, you can start training right away. If the female cria has been born on your ranch, you can begin prior to weaning at four months. The male crias should not be started until after weaning to be sure that they don't imprint on humans, although naturally we weigh them and treat them for any medical emergency. Most llamas are weaned between five and six months; crias of old dams are weaned earlier, and those nursing from overweight dams may be weaned later.

HALTER-TRAINING

Halter-training is the most important step in your llama's education. He must be taught to accept the halter as early as possible, without any fuss.

Walk into the corral with the halter and lead rope in sight; your llama will quickly learn that this is his time to work. Avoid chasing your llama or he will be nervous and tired before you even begin. An assistant who can aid you in catching your pupil is invaluable.

Begin training sessions when your llama is about four months of age.

Slowly slip the halter over the llama's nose.

Take your time so that the message is clear.

Finally, secure the poll strap.

When your llama has explored all avenues of escape and knows he's trapped, he'll freeze. Put your arm around his neck very slowly, talking to him constantly in a soothing tone. Reassure him, but be on the alert for a sudden lunge or leap. Sometimes he'll dance nervously; as long as he moves, don't be too concerned. It's the frozen, rigid llama, quivering like a taut strand of wire, who is most likely to bolt. If you have an assistant, he should stand in a position to block any chance of escape.

The llama's first instinct is to run away from you or foreign objects. When catching a llama without assistance, some owners hold a long stick or crop extended from each arm to help corner the llama. Talk to him reassuringly and calmly. Your demeanor should be matter-of-fact but not threatening; act as if this is something you do everyday and that you intend to succeed.

Gently rub your hand up and down the llama's neck, saying, "Good boy!" After he begins to accept your handling, and starts to relax, let him go. However, do so slowly so that he knows you are giving him permission and that he isn't initiating his own freedom. Repeat this activity several times a day until he knows that he won't be harmed in any way. Don't rush things; do this exercise for about three days.

On the fourth or fifth day introduce the halter. Work slowly, letting him see and smell it first. Very gently work the halter over his nose. When he accepts it without a fight, remove it as a reward. When training, we use a quick snap to avoid fumbling and to minimize the chances of escape. The quick snap is very similar to the clip that is found on some dog leashes. Located on the cheek strap, it is simple to slip over the ring and snap in place. Do not use the quick snap when the llama is off the premises as the snap itself is not very strong and we have had it release under pressure.

Continue to put the halter on and off over the nose until he is relaxed. When he seems bored, it's time to fasten the cheek strap. Let the halter stay on without any hand pressure for about fifteen minutes, then take it off again as a reward. After a few days, he'll start to put his nose in it without hesitation. Then you know it's time for the next lesson.

Never yank or jerk the halter off quickly, as your llama will associate this with shaking or throwing his head to be free. Always take the time to remove it slowly, while your arm is still around his neck. You are letting him go, not vice versa.

TRAINING TO LEAD

As your llama is still skittish, have an assistant stand next to him, opposite you, to help hold him if necessary. Place a loose-fitting 25" leather buckle dog collar around the base of the llama's neck at the shoulder, to give you something to grip if he panics. This also helps to avoid unnecessary strain on that long young neck.

Attach the lead rope to the halter and gently but firmly pull forward and give a consistently used command like "Come!" Keep applying pressure until he steps forward. The second he moves, release the pressure and praise him. This is called the "tug and release" system. As long as the llama is moving forward, do not pull on the lead rope, and praise him constantly. When he does stop, pull on the lead again until he moves.

Your llama may decide to buck and rear at any time during this process. Don't be alarmed; this is normal. Grab the collar, and don't allow him to thrash and injure you or himself. Talk slowly and soothingly. If he decides to "kush" (sit down), put your foot under his chest and point your toe upward, while saying "Up!" loudly.

Kushing is a llama's way of saying, "I've had enough." You don't want him to get in the habit of doing this. Your helper may have to reach down and tickle his rear legs. Keep repeating the command "Up!" until he obeys. Then praise him.

Keep in mind that no two llamas are alike. They will differ in the rate at which they learn. Some take longer to teach to lead, while others master it in one or two lessons. If your animal balks like a mule, tug his head forward and pull it from side to side. This puts him off balance and forces him to take a step. When he moves, release the pull and praise. Sometimes it only takes having someone walk around behind him while you are pulling. In the first stages of training, llamas don't like someone to approach them from behind. Continue this exercise until he walks willingly at your side.

You know a llama is well-trained when he steps out in a lively manner next to you, and is more interested in the passing scenery than in fighting the lead rope. But a new problem commonly arises at this point. He becomes too eager and wants to take off ahead of you. To stop this, extend your arm in front of his chest, or put your hand in front of his face. To lead the llama properly, position your body at his left side so that you are ear to ear. Some backpackers

Once lead trained, llamas are easy to handle. Photo copyright
Pedes Oberg, 1985. *Courtesy Jay and Karen Stager.*

prefer that the llama walks behind them; this is up to you. The ear
to ear position is preferred in the show ring.

With practice, he will actually become an enthusiastic walking companion. He will stroll along next to you, sightseeing, even humming
from time to time.

DESENSITIZING

Llamas and alpacas are creatures of flight, which means that their
main line of defense is to run from an enemy. Thus they count on
their legs, which are extremely sensitive. If you were to grab his leg,
the llama's immediate response would be to leap backward or fold it
under and away from you. They will even sit down or "kush." At
this stage of training the llama must be desensitized so that you can
touch all parts of its body.

Brushing

Grooming is probably most effective in this process; besides building
a trust level, you help maintain a healthy and lustrous coat. Start
brushing in the neck area and gradually move down the back and

Keep your hand pressure firm but gentle as you gradually move your hand down the chest and forelegs.

Talk to your llama as you stroke all the way to the toes.

sides. I count my success in inches. The first day, do only the back and sides — you may not get even this far. The second day I start working on the chest, and on the third, I move to the top of the forelegs. At this point, I remove the brush and use only my hands. With firm and steady pressure, I work my hand down a few inches in a gentle stroking action. When the llama becomes tense, I slide my hand back up, never removing it from his body. When he relaxes, I move my hand down again, hopefully further than last time. When he has allowed you to go further and is relaxed, give him a break.

Lifting the Feet

Finally, success! You can rub your hand all the way down to his front toes, and it's time to lift a foot. Slide your hand down to just below the knee and gently wrap your fingers around the leg. Don't worry if the llama becomes agitated; don't let go unless absolutely necessary. He will struggle; when he stops pulling away, lift the leg backward and up so that you can view the bottom of the pad. Hold the leg in this position for a few seconds, praising him throughout,

Slide your hand down the leg and wrap your fingers firmly around the cannon bone.

Lift the leg, hold it up briefly, then lower the foot back to the ground.

and then firmly place the foot back on the ground. Let him know that you are in control. Repeat this lesson three or four times each day until this activity becomes ordinary. Lifting the rear feet should only be done after you have desensitized the rear legs. Llamas cow-kick in a movement to the side which is very accurate.

An animal that permits you to lift his feet is a joy to own. Trimming nails is far easier, and on the trail you will be able to inspect the feet for injury.

Desensitizing the Posterior

Being able to handle your llama's rear legs may take a little longer because of the possibility that he will kick. A riding crop, length of narrow PCV pipe or just a plain broom handle are useful tools for this exercise.

Holding the lead rope in your left hand, face the llama's posterior and rub the crop gently but firmly down his rump. Methodically and slowly, repeat the exercises you did on the forelegs. Llamas "cowkick" to the side, and while not as dangerous as a horse that kicks, they can inflict injury. If he does kick, hold the crop firmly in place while talking soothingly to him until he stops, then move it down the leg again. Once he has accepted a foreign object on his legs, use your hands. Lift the rear feet up under the llama just as you did the foreleg.

Using a Blower for Desensitizing

One of the best investments you can make is an air blower. Leaf blowers used in landscape cleanup are good, as well as various commercial grooming blowers. They effectively fast-dry your llama, remove the debris from his coat and are excellent for desensitizing.

Introduce the blower cautiously, or you may find out how high a llama can jump. Let him see and smell it before you turn it on. Pointing it away from him, turn it on the lowest setting. Slowly let the nozzle drift toward the neck and gradually move it over the entire body. Don't direct the air toward the legs until the llama has accepted the sensation on his body.

Because it puts forth steady air pressure the llama can't evade, a blower is extremely effective in desensitizing the rear legs. It may take a few days before you can apply air to the coat. At first condition him to the sound of the motor; then depending on his response, begin applying air directly to the coat. After several days of grooming with a blower, you will be amazed at how much your llama likes it. He may actually come to you when it's on.

CORRECTING A "SPITTER"

You may have purchased a llama that already spits, or your weanling may develop this nasty habit as he matures (most crias don't spit). Remember, llamas are territorial, and you are invading their space as you approach. When your llama first spits, he may be testing you. Don't react with a loud voice; after all, the substance washes off easily and won't stain clothing. Reprimand him in a firm and moderate tone of voice. Make it clear that his behavior is unacceptable. Then continue what you were doing. If you stop at this stage, he will have won and will spit again when he doesn't want to comply with your requests.

If he spits again, tie a handkerchief over his nose with the ends attached to the rings of the halter. Next time, he'll have to suffer the smell of his own spit, which is highly unpleasant. I have used a water pistol, spraying it into the spitting llama's face. You may have to try both tactics with a persistent spitter. Each time you discipline him, reinforce the action with "NO!" In short, try to nip this habit in the bud. The sooner you confront the problem, the easier it will be to resolve.

TRANSPORTING

"Have llama, will travel" is something that every llama owner aspires to. If you want to show or backpack, or transport your llama for breeding, it is essential to be able to haul him. In addition, it's less expensive to take your llama to the vet instead of paying for a ranch call. If you plan to visit schools or promote llamas in any other way, trailering will be an important lesson.

Training to Load

Since we enjoy our llama's company as we travel, we use a standard-sized van. If you have a trailer the same lessons will apply.

Start when your llama is young, as he will be easier to lift. If possible, even before he's weaned, hoist him into the van a few times so that it's not so frightening later. As with other training, having a helper or two is optimum. Approach the vehicle slowly and allow your pupil to sniff and explore. Take your time.

Open the door to permit further exploration. The llama will usually poke his head inside and warily eyeball the interior. Have one assistant climb inside and hold the end of the lead rope. The other person should walk up behind the llama casually to block him from the rear. Standing beside the llama, talk softly to him, encouraging him to "Jump!" While you pull on the lead rope, the person at the rear should lean against the llama's hindquarters. If you're lucky, he'll hop in. Most of the time, though, he will plant his feet and balk.

Be careful that his forelegs don't wedge under the bottom of the van; lean down slowly and take the left foreleg in your hand, below the knee. Lift the leg and place it on the step or inside the trailer. As you do this, your helper should push the llama forward. You may have to actually lift him up and in, easiest when the animal is young.

Once he's inside, the hardest work is over. Most young llamas will stand still and shake, frozen to the spot. Praise him and talk to him until he relaxes. He should stay in the trailer or van for at least ten minutes. Once he starts sniffing and looking around, you're over the hurdle.

Turn him around, open the doors, and let him jump out. Be very careful that you don't permit him to take a "flying leap" or he could injure himself. We stand on both sides of the door and keep his head down with the lead rope so that he is under control and looks where he's going. Repeat the lesson immediately, while everything is fresh in his mind. Do this at least three times; if your back can hold out, four is even better. Each time will be easier. Take him for a short walk

Encourage the llama to inspect the vehicle before attempting to load him.

You can train a llama to load without an assistant if you take plenty
of time and give lots of encouragement.

Don't allow the llama's legs to dig in.

He's ready to take the plunge!

afterwards as a reward. After the first day, you will need to load once or twice a day to firmly implant the message. In one week he should hop in with very little encouragement, and you'll be ready to take a ride!

Hitting the Road

Just go around the block on your first trip, as you don't want to stress your llama too much. Gradually lengthen the rides. Most llamas will first stand and lean into the curves, finally giving up and kushing on the floorboards. Remember when using a trailer do not tie them, since they do like to sit.

On longer trips if the llama becomes unduly nervous and restless, he may need to relieve himself. We try to take care of this before we start the trip. Remember to carry pellets in a covered container for an emergency.

On your jaunts, have a destination in mind, and be cautious when you arrive. Survey the area to make sure there are no loose dogs or crowds. Bring a secure halter and lead rope with you. Don't stop along a freeway, as a llama could bolt into the traffic; pull well off the road. Rest areas are not good environments for llamas either; you'll be amazed at the commotion you can cause and how fast a crowd may assemble.

Carry food and water only if it is a hot day or you plan on being gone for a long time. For jaunts around town, we wait to feed and water when we get home.

TRAINING TO PACK

Just as the retriever is in his glory with the hunter, the llama goes lead in hand with the hiker. These gentle companions were born to pack. Once the llama has accepted the strange contraption on his back, he is eager to head out.

After you've trained your llama to lead, load and unload, it is time to introduce him to weight on his back. Start with a towel or light-weight blanket. We don't secure these initially but merely let them lie on his back. If we are working with a weanling, we never put weight on his back; we just want him to know something is there.

After the llama is a year old, we advance our training. The bag that paper boys deliver newspapers in is an excellent teaching device; it has a pouch on both sides and can be draped over the llama. By attaching strings to the bag, we can secure it under the llama's chest.

Then we add a little weight, like wrapped sandwiches and a few soft drinks. Your llama may dance around a bit, but usually doesn't fight the weight for long. Reward him with alfalfa pellets. When you introduce him to the trail, take someone else with you, along with another llama if possible. Llamas like to have one of their own kind with them; it makes a day-hike more enjoyable for everyone.

Most backpackers refrain from adding heavy weight until their llamas are three years old. Keep in mind that they are still growing up to this point, and that you could injure their somewhat delicate vertebrae.

Types of Packs

There are basically two types of packs, soft and hard. There has been a great deal of controversy within the industry as to the merits of each. For the owner just starting out, I would recommend the soft pack. The hard pack consists of a pad, a frame and packs which attach to the frame. The packs are called panniers. The soft pack has a heavy pad with snaps to which the panniers are attached. In general the soft pack is easier to use. I bring the panniers inside the house to pack them more efficiently and weigh them out for more balance.

Regardless of which you use, attachments or ties are similar. A chest band keeps the pack from sliding back. There are two cinches, one for behind the shoulder, the other for under the stomach. A rear band that fits around the rump keeps the pack from slipping forward. Use care in attaching the back cinch near the stomach so that it doesn't rub against the penis. If your llama has been well desensitized, it will be easy to secure these straps.

The age and size of your llama will determine how much he can carry. At one year of age, the llama is still growing and the vertebrae can be easily damaged with too heavy a load. I would recommend no more than fifteen to twenty pounds total, INCLUDING the pack and saddle frame — fifteen pounds for the smaller llama and twenty for a larger llama of the same age. At age two years, the load can be increased to twenty-five to thirty pounds, depending on the size, and at three years of age when the llama is considered an adult, the total weight can be fifty to sixty pounds. Don't be in a rush to load these guys. Remember, the more comfortable the llama is, the more he too will enjoy the trip.

The Stake-Out Line

The llama also needs to become familiar with a stake-out line. The stake can be purchased at most pet stores. It has a large screw at the

Position the pack saddle first, then secure the chest strap.

The front cinch fits just behind the elbow.

The rear cinch should fit just behind the rib area and should
not rub on the penis.

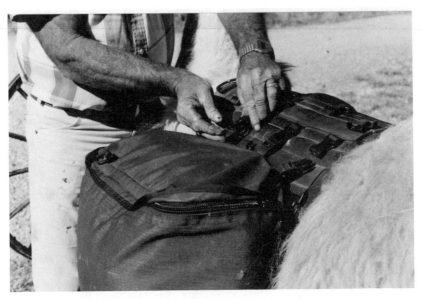

Snapping the panniers on is easy. Pictured are Boony Doon* packs.

bottom and a round swivel loop at the top. The llama is tied to the stake with approximately twenty feet of soft rope. Once the stake is screwed into the ground, the llama can graze in a large circular area. As a precaution, we tie a bicycle inner tube to the stake. The rope is then tied to the inner tube. This allows for flexibility in the lead line. If the llama were to panic and lunge quickly, the inner tube prevents a sudden hard jerk to the neck and head.

Llamas quickly learn to maneuver around the stake and not get caught up in the lead rope. However this does take practice and should be learned at home. Once when Cheech was tied to a tree in the front yard I noticed he was kushed up close to the tree. On investigation, I saw that the rope was wrapped around him several times. Trying not to panic him, I slowly moved up and released him by the halter snap. I was amazed at how patiently he allowed me to unravel the mess. He knew he was in trouble and I was the one to free him. When the rope was loose again, he got up and resumed grazing as if nothing had happened, and to this day has never wrapped himself up again.

Day Hikes

The best way to get started in packing is to begin with day hikes, beginning early morning and returning before sunset. The load should be light and equipment minimal. Choose a park or recreation area that is close to home. Call the park service or ranger to make sure that llamas are permitted and that the trails are open and in good condition. Try to visit an area with a variety of topography, such as streams, hillsides and meadows. This will all be a training area plus an enjoyable trip. Whether you plan on going alone with your llama, (I don't recommend this practice) or taking along other companions, always let someone know where you are planning to go, your route and your estimated time of return. Inexperienced hikers can become easily disoriented and lost. When you call the ranger or park service personnel for permission on the llamas, it is also wise to let them know how many "hearts" are in your party. "Hearts" mean the total number of hikers AND livestock.

If you are not familiar with the area, take a map and a compass. A long lead rope and a stake will permit you to take a breather along the way. Since you will probably only need a lunch, take sandwiches, fruit, cheese and crackers. Pelleted alfalfa makes a good lunch for the llama, in addition to the browsing he will do during the breaks. For day hiking, we take along a wide variety of juices and a canteen of water from home. Small coolers will fit in the panniers and will keep

Llamas on a tether line.

The last ten minutes of a six-day pack trip! *Courtesy the Barkmans.*

your drinks and sandwiches chilled. We freeze some of the juices the night before. The frozen containers help to keep the coolers cold.

Most important is the first aid kit (see First Aid chapter). Duct tape is particularly important as we use it to tape gauze pads to llama foot pads that have been cut on sharp rocks.

Loading the Packs

Llamas will kush on the trail and refuse to move if the packs are off balance. Imagine yourself walking along the trail with twenty pounds in your left hand and thirty pounds in you right. With the frame pack, it may be more difficult for the inexperienced packer to balance the weight. For this reason you need a scale similar to the hanging fish scales.

Weigh the saddle and the pack frame, if you are using one. Remember the frame must also be added into the total weight. Pack your supplies into the pannier, distributing the weight evenly. Place the heavier items in the bottom of the panniers so that this weight will hang lower on the llama's side. This technique helps to keep the pack from twisting and turning the saddle during the trip. Then weigh each pannier, making sure the weight is even on each side. Each pannier is then snapped or buckled to the saddle when you are prepared to take off at the trail head.

On the Trail

Some llamas are born leaders while others are content to bring up the rear. If your llama is constantly pushing forward, you may want to try him in the lead position. Vice versa, if your lead llama is constantly lagging, move him behind. Once the pattern is established, everyone should move along comfortably.

In the beginning, the llamas may spook a little when the packs brush against branches and shrubs. Gradually they will become accustomed to this, even moving aside to avoid contact.

Since llamas are herd oriented and very social, they often become distressed when other llamas are out of sight, therefore it is easier to pack with two or more animals. Inexperienced packers will become almost frantic until they see the other llamas. Talk to your buddy, keeping him calm if you become separated from the others in your group.

First time packers will sometimes simply stop on the trail and kush. The reasons are varied. They may be unsure — suddenly the home pasture is more appealing. They may be tired, or the load isn't balanced. Whatever the reason, try to get the llama up (so you don't

The Barkman's packing a string of llamas.

create bad habits). If he won't get up, move the rest of the llamas out of sight and he will quickly change his mind. Move to a rest area and see if there is a problem with the pack. If you have been walking for a while it might be time to take a break. The more trips you take, the more you will become attuned to the llama. If he suddenly stops and stares into the trees, look and see what has caught his attention. Usually a ground squirrel or other form of wildlife has intrigued him. Enjoy it with him before you press on. My llamas will constantly hum and often point out things that I would normally overlook.

Obstacles Along the Way

Go out of your way to tackle a few obstacles. After all, you are training. A downed log is a challenge: try to get the llama to jump it. He will soon get the feel of the pack lightening and then landing down on his back. Duck under the trees and wind around them. Within hours, the llama will learn that he has to allow room for the pack and sidestep accordingly.

When approaching steep hillsides, be sure to give him enough lead rope going up the hill so that he can maneuver. However, when going downhill, keep your hand closer to the halter and hold his head down.

He has to see where he is going and you want to avoid wild leaps. Always go slowly downhill and keep the llama under control. Loose shale and rock can cause both of you to slip and slide.

Ravines and washouts pose another challenge. Don't let your llama get into the habit of leaping. He could be landing on soft soil or he could injure himself on sharp rocks. Always keep his head down and lead him down and across.

Creeks and streams always provide a refreshing drink for the llamas, however running water tends to have the same effect on llamas that it does on children. A llama allowed to stand in the water will want to defecate and urinate, which is not pleasant for anyone downstream. When entering the water, keep the llama moving through it. Once he is on the other side, you can lead him away from the water to take care of business and then return for a clean drink. Even though we do not drink the water ourselves, we do allow the llamas to refresh themselves. I am not aware of giardia problems in llamas, although it may be possible. If streams and creeks are not on your trek you need to carry ample water for your llama, and also a few "raisins" in a jar to encourage defecation during the rest stops.

Sometimes llamas are hesitant to walk in water, especially if they are unfamiliar with ponds or streams. As in any training, you will have to accustom them to this. Usually, when one foot is in, the rest is easy. Our Calvin loves the water and will kush and even swim if given the chance.

At the turn-around point of your trip, take a long break. Remove the packs from the llamas, stake them out and feed them a lunch of alfalfa pellets. While they're grazing, break out your own lunch and enjoy!

Be aware of poisonous plants in your area and be conscious of what the llamas are munching. (see chapter 5). Also be considerate of the environment. Don't tie the llama to a young sapling that could be stripped of its foliage within minutes. Avoid camping in fragile meadows where the fresh vegetation could be forever trampled.

Llamas have minimal impact in the wilderness areas and their feces closely resemble that of elk. Unlike pack mules and horses, which definitely leave their mark, one can hardly tell a llama has passed through the area.

Horses and Pack Mules on the Trail
Rarely will you find yourself alone on your trip. If the area is visited often by other hikers, you may run into horses and pack mules. Many horses have never seen a llama and may spook at the sight of one.

No one wants to have a rider thrown or packs strewn along the trail. Whenever we are on the trail, we are constantly alert for the sound of approaching horses. If encountered, one of us will go ahead and inform the riders of our presence, while the others in our group take the llamas off the trail and into the trees. It's always amusing to see the horses pass us by, wide eyed and snorting while the llamas stare with curiosity, munching all the time.

Llamas are relatively new to the wilderness areas and it is important for good public relations to show courtesy to other packers and avoid confrontation on the trails. More and more national parks and recreation areas are opening for llamas where horses are not allowed. Minimal trace packing is the reason. So promote llamas while on the trail, foster good relations with horse and mule packers, and be considerate of others who seek the peace, solitude and beauty of the great outdoors.

Overnight and Longer Pack Trips

If you are planning on undertaking many long trips into wilderness areas, you should first join a commercial pack trip with experienced llama packers. The knowledge you gain will teach you far more than any book. A list of commercial packers is located in the appendix.

However, if you feel confident enough to tackle a few overnights on the trail, the following may be helpful.

Most of all, the llamas, your companions and YOU must be in top physical condition. Forestry and park personnel should be contacted for permission and information regarding the trail conditions. They should be notified regarding the "hearts" in your party and your destination. Remember to let someone at home know where you're going. You will require more equipment and supplies.

Take enough clothing for the time you plan. Rain gear is essential as mountain weather can change. A sleeping bag and tent can be attached to the tops of the packs with bungee cords.

Visit your local sports shops and surplus stores to round out the inventory you will need. As you purchase, keep weight constantly in mind. Fortunately for llama enthusiasts, you are not limited to the freeze-dried foods of the backpacker. Since the llamas can pack so much in, you can enjoy delicious meals with fresh meat, vegetables and fruit.

Your camp should be free of any poisonous plants which the llamas could eat. Make sure the spot is large enough to stake them, or use a picket line (a long rope tied between two trees). Loops are set in the rope every eight to ten feet. The llamas can then be secured to

Don coordinates pressure on the lead rope with Tristin's direction on the reins.

the loops by their lead ropes. Grassy areas will keep them happy and supplement the alfalfa pellets.

Always be alert for nervousness with the llamas. They may be signaling to you that a forest creature is near. First time packers may be nervous away from the barn. As they become more experienced, they will settle in and become a permanent fixture on your future hikes.

RIDING A LLAMA

A llama can carry only one fourth of his body weight; therefore, children are the best candidates for riding. After your llama has experience carrying a pack, it isn't difficult to add a child to the list. When your youngster takes his or her first ride, have assistants on either side of the llama while you remain at the head. Lift the child on gently, and praise the llama. Then lead him forward for several steps. At first he may try to rear or kush; but proceed slowly, talking to him.

It takes skill and patience to teach a llama to pull a cart. Betty Barkman driving Boots.

Reins may be added to the halter cheek rings. Once you feel confident that the llama will accept his rider, you can accompany him, coordinating the lead rope with the rider's use of the reins. The rider should also use "Come" and "Stop."

Some llamas adapt to being ridden sooner than others, depending on their personality. Recognize and accept these variables in your llamas, and make a wise choice about which to use for this purpose.

Llamas can also be trained to pull carts and maneuver through difficult obstacle courses. Don't be afraid to tackle new challenges with your llamas. The more you do with him, the healthier and happier he will be.

CHAPTER TEN

EXHIBITING YOUR LLAMA

After years of carefully planned breeding, and after months of training your llama progeny, you scrutinize the cria before you and ask, "Did we do well? Or am I biased?"

There are divergent opinions about shows; some are opposed to setting "standards" because we are still learning about camelids in general. But for others the central question has become, "What is the correct llama?" These breeders feel there is a need for guidelines in llama breeding programs to avoid trends or fads that would take away from llamas in future generations.

Perhaps one of the most significant articles written on the "ideal" llama is by Dr. Murray E. Fowler, D.V.M. In this article, "Form, Function, Conformation and Soundness," in the November/December, 1986 issue of *Llamas Magazine*, Dr. Fowler clearly stated that the llama's functions are directly related to conformation, and judges use these guidelines today. However, since there are still no formally established standards for size, wool length, weight or other features, some llama organizations have elected to have performance shows only. They support activities such as packing competitions, obstacle courses and cart-driving.

GETTING INVOLVED

Showing is a way to compare your llama with others in your area and have fun at the same time. Llamas are exhibited at expos, county and state fairs and other events. Most shows are open to the public and provide those interested in llamas with an opportunity to promote their own animals and ranch, as well as to network and share experiences with other breeders.

Llasa's Snow Princess, 1987 Grand Champion female,
California State Fair.

Many youth groups, such as 4-H and FFA, are joining the llama
craze. The llama's size and disposition make him an excellent youth
project.

SHOW-SPONSORING ORGANIZATIONS

The two leading llama organizations, the ILA and LANA, have
similar purposes: to educate members and the public about llamas
and to advance and promote the interests of the industry as a whole.

The International Llama Association (ILA) has regional conferences
where members can attend workshops and exhibit their llamas in
various activities. As of this writing ILA sponsors performance classes
only. The membership is notified of locales and dates via newsletter.
Local chapters of ILA sponsor shows and get-togethers where members can exhibit.

The Llama Association of North America (LANA) sponsors expos
that are like conventions lasting four or five days. The first days are
devoted to workshops, veterinary panels, and speakers, while the
last two days are reserved for shows.

The show is divided into halter and performance competition. Good conformation and wool quality are the goals of the halter divisions, whereas the object of the performance class is to show how well the llama performs on simulated trails and in a crowd.

The American Llama Show Association (ALSA) sanctions shows that have both halter and performance classes. The halter classes are divided into various age groups and wool lengths: short wool for llamas with minimal fiber on the body; medium wool for llamas with abundant fiber on the body but not on the face and legs; and long wool for llamas with abundant wool on the face, legs and body. Exhibitors are allowed to determine which classes to show in, but the judge may move the animal to a different classification at his or her discretion.

In order for a llama to achieve championship status in the ALSA, he is required to compete against a minimum of four contestants per class, be registered, and the owner must be a member of ALSA. A total of 35 points earned in both halter and performance classes are required. The number of points earned for each win depends on the number of animals in the class. If you are the only entry, you would not receive any points. Championships can be awarded at other shows such as state fairs, county fairs and expos not associated with ALSA by winning at all levels of competition with the top award being "Champion" or best of that show.

PREPARATION

Health Requirements
Whenever you transport llamas over state lines be aware of the health requirements of the destination state. If you pass through other states on the way to your destination, agricultural inspection stations will want to see your documentation. Have your veterinarian check these requirements for you. Practically every state requires a health certificate to have been completed within thirty days of the transport date and signed by your veterinarian. Your home state will also require this for reentry into the state, so be sure when showing that you will be returning within thirty days.

Some states require additional certification that the animal is free from tuberculosis, brucellosis or blue tongue disease, and that there is no evidence of scabies or lice. Tuberculosis testing involves an injection under the tail and a check for reaction within 72 hours. The brucellosis test consists of a blood sample that is submitted to a state laboratory for analysis. As lab results take time, don't wait until the last minute.

Show Equipment

You can buy halters from llama suppliers listed in llama publications, feed stores can order them, or you can have them made by harness-makers. Sizes for crias, medium and large-sized animals are available. A llama's head grows rapidly, so the halters should be adjustable. The halter fits properly if the nose strap is fairly close to the eyes so that it won't slip down the bridge of the nose and choke off the nostrils. A correct fit will be snug but not tight. You should be able to slip one finger under the straps. Stay away from halters that have straps wider than three quarter inch and those with large, heavy hardware. The llama's face is delicate, and heavy halters distract from the features and are uncomfortable. The halter should be sleek but strong, made of either leather or nylon. I prefer nylon, since I can throw it in the washing machine. Avoid anything that might detract from your llama's face, such as gaudy colors or tassels. These items should be reserved for costume shows.

When you travel to a show or expo, you'll also need to take along the following items:

rake
shovel
hose
watering buckets
bedding and feed
first aid kit
fans (in hot weather)
dry shampoo (for emergency cleanup)
blower
display materials
hammer, nails, tacks, etc.
brushes and slickers
table and chairs
business cards
extra halter(s) and lead ropes
towels
health certificates

Attire and Grooming

When llama afficionado first started showing, they dressed in every conceivable outfit. We would see shorts and shower thongs, Peruvian ponchos and even tuxedos. Today the industry has come a long way; partly due to criticism by other livestock groups. References were made to "those crazy llama folks that didn't even know how to dress in the ring." Today, if you attend a state fair, you'll see 4-Hers in neat uniforms, and adults in suits and ties.

Dark colors such as navy blue, black or dark browns slacks with matching vest or jacket that contrast with your llama are appropriate, with a light colored shirt or blouse. Women should wear slacks or skirts (not too short). Remember that you are trying to show your animal at his best.

Long haired exhibitors should tie or pin their hair to prevent it from covering up the exhibitor number pinned to the back of their blouse or shirt.

In performance classes, the dress code is more relaxed. Since you will be climbing over obstacles, your clothing needs to be comfortable and unrestrictive. Shorts, slacks and tennis shoes are appropriate.

Groom your llama to perfection, trimming his toenails, and making sure his coat is free of mats. Be prepared to brush for hours. It takes about six weeks of frequent brushing to bring a llama's coat to optimum show condition. Some exhibitors use cornstarch or grooming powder to aid in brushing out dirt and tangles. Static can be eliminated by spraying diluted fabric softener on the coat and brushing it in. Arrive early for your first show and watch how the pros groom their animals.

Most breeders like to decorate their stalls with ranch banners, flowers and other festive items such as photographs, educational and promotional materials, genealogies and ribbons. Many shows award prizes for the most attractive displays, and for the cleanest stalls; the latter are sometimes referred to as "herdsman awards."

AT THE SHOW

When you first arrive, you will need to check in with the registration booth, have the show vet or barn manager check your papers and locate your stall(s). Once everyone is settled and you've met your neighbors, look over the program to see when your classes are scheduled. Most exhibitors arrive the night before the show so everyone can get a good night's sleep. Halter classes normally start off the show and begin around 9:00 a.m., with the performance classes the following day. During the night your show prospect may have soiled himself and require some serious touching up. Therefore, you need to allow at least one hour before your class to put on the finishing touches.

There is nothing more frustrating than having your llama defecate in the ring; it seems to set a pattern for all the other llamas. So about a half hour before the class, take him for a walk and try to find a dung pile. Many gate keepers will establish a dung pile near the ring for just this purpose. If the llama has relieved himself before entering the ring, he'll show better and step out livelier. Incidentally, if he does happen to have an accident in the ring later, don't panic. Just stop until he has finished, and cover up the droppings with sawdust or other material as a courtesy to the other competitors.

Numbers are provided in the registration package, and will be your only identity in the ring. At the entrance to every show ring you'll find a gate person whose duty it is to line up the exhibitors in numerical order, answer questions, see that everyone is present and wearing a number, and briefly instruct all on how to enter the ring.

The ring steward's duty is to assist the judge and the competitors. The judge tells the steward how he plans to handle the class, and how he would like the exhibitors to conduct themselves. The steward is essentially a intermediary between you and the judge. When it's time for the class, the judge will nod to the ring steward, who in turn tells the gate person. The lineup is then asked to enter the ring and the first person asked to begin to circle it, usually counter-clockwise. Each competitor follows the person in front of him, keeping a distance of approximately six to eight feet. The judge stands in the center of the circle to take note of each llama.

Halter Classes

According to LANA guidelines, the judges of halter classes look for best in group, and rate competitors on a scale of one to five or six. In order to reach their decisions, the judges take both positive and negative traits into account.

Walk ear to ear with your llama, and try to keep a loose lead. Don't appear to be dragging your companion. After you have circled the ring once or twice (depending on the number of entries), the ring steward will ask everyone to reverse direction so that he can see the llama's other side. After the judge has gaited the llamas, he'll line you up along the ring side, llamas facing the center. The judge then walks up and down the line, looking at the llamas from the front. Judges' procedures vary. Usually but not always, the judge positions himself on the far side of the ring and asks each exhibitor to walk his llama toward him, one by one.

When the judge has walked down the line and it's your turn, he'll motion to you. Lead your llama, at a walk, to a point approximately

Tristin presents the llama to Judge John Mallon.

In performance classes, llamas may be asked to cross bridges.

six feet from the judge, and stop. He may ask a few questions and will move around, studying your llama from all sides. He may want to feel the llama's back or other parts of his body. When finished, he will ask you to return to the line. Turn your llama to the right in a tight turn (called a "haunch turn," almost a pivot) and jog back to the line. The judge will observe the llama's leg movement and gait at the faster pace. This is important, since in many instances a leg defect will not show up until an animal is in motion.

After the judge has inspected each entry, he will review his notes and place the winners. Whether you win or don't place at all, be gracious and a good sport.

If you plan to exhibit your llamas, attend a few shows to study ring procedure, and pay particular attention to showmanship classes to watch the handlers perfect their techniques.

Remember that no two judges are alike. They must judge what they see in the ring on a particular day. Another day may be different; the llama may be better behaved and show better. There are many variables. Some judges prefer to see leaner llamas and will discount a llama if he is just a few pounds overweight, while others like to see large, athletic llamas. If you show often, you'll get to know the different judges' preferences.

Don't be discouraged if your animal doesn't place. Tomorrow is another day. View each show as a training experience, and keep it enjoyable.

LLAMA ASSOCIATION OF NORTH AMERICA
CONFORMATION GUIDELINES

Overall Appearance:	The Llama should be well-proportioned, balanced and symmetrical.
Head:	The head should be carried proudly, in an alert manner. The jaw formation should encourage correct bite and dentition.
Front legs:	The front legs should be relatively straight with generally forward-facing toes and properly angled pasterns. There should be good bone density.
Rear legs:	The rear legs should be relatively straight from hock to fetlock joint when viewed from the side or rear. The toes

	should be generally forward-facing and the pasterns should be properly angled. There should be good bone density.
Movement:	In a pacing gait, all limbs should move freely and smoothly.
Wool:	The wool should have a healthy lustre.
Reproductive Organs:	The testicles should both be visible and appear uniform. The female genitalia should be normal-appearing.
Disposition:	A good disposition is highly desirable. (Such disposition is reflected by a calm animal; he should stand quietly and permit the judge to touch his body. Spitting or kicking are definitely bad habits. The llama should be alert, and willing to step out quickly and enthusiastically.)

Anything can happen at a show. Once, while competing in a halter class, I noticed that Calvin was warily eyeing the judge and almost staring. Calvin had been in many shows and was always a model llama; I could count on him to be well-mannered. As we circled the ring, Calvin started to lag. I whispered, "Come on, Calvin, what's wrong?" as I felt him becoming tense.

The ring steward motioned for us to line up and the judge walked up the line, standing across the ring from me. He was very friendly, which helped to relax the exhibitors, but certainly not Calvin. When he asked me to walk my llama forward, I had a mule on my hands! Calvin refused to get near the judge! I literally dragged him to the required position.

Assuming the role of "Rebel Without a Cause," Calvin stood with feet planted and ears far back. The judge walked up to us and asked if he could touch my llama. Not wanting to appear intimidated by this spoiled child next to me, I said yes.

Shock set in when I realized what was going to happen next. As the judge put his hand on Calvin's back, he quickly and deliberately turned his head, aimed and fired. The judge was now sporting a green jacket! I apologized profusely, trying to tell him that Calvin never acted like this. The victim reassured me that it was o.k., and proceeded to circle behind Calvin. Then the final blow occurred. With a lightening flash, he KICKED! I wanted to be swallowed up in the sawdust. The judge made a few notes and continued down the line. The remaining time in the class was agony. Calvin continued to maintain his defiant stance until it was time to leave the ring.

The minute we left the gate and started back to the stall, his attitude changed completely. Up went the ears, his step was lively, and he even hummed a few bars! We have never had this experience again.

Showmanship Classes

The American Llama Show Association's handbook describes showmanship class as a "demonstration of the handler's ability to show (his) animal to its best advantage at halter. Judging is based on the exhibitor's basic skills in fitting, grooming, and style of presenting the animal. Conformation is not considered. The handler's attire must be neat, clean and appropriate for the class.

Classes are usually divided into several categories: Adult, nineteen years and older; Intermediate, thirteen to eighteen years; Junior, twelve years and younger. Novice and maiden classes may be included; novice meaning one who has not won more than three blue ribbons, and maiden for those who have never won a blue ribbon.

The class procedure is similar to that of the halter classes and the judge should post a diagram near the entrance to the ring so that exhibitors can familiarize themselves with the required pattern. In general, a showmanship class is more formal, with the exhibitors putting their best foot forward. Some important rules to keep in mind are: keep your eye on your llama and the judge; never position yourself between the two or block the judge's view; when standing, make sure that the llama is standing firmly on all four feet. Follow directions and pay attention.

4-H or Future Farmers of America (FFA) are some of the best classes to watch, as these youth spend many hours practicing their showmanship techniques, and are good examples for all of us.

Performance Classes

Watching a llama do what he is best at is one of the most rewarding parts of a show. There are numerous entertaining and rewarding classes in which your llama can show off his agility, versatility and worthiness as a trail or hiking companion.

Obstacle Classes — The purpose of the obstacle class is to demonstrate the well-trained llama's obedience and willingness to go where his handler asks him. Obstacles are designed to resemble what a pack llama would meet on the trail: bridges, ponds, piles of fallen logs,

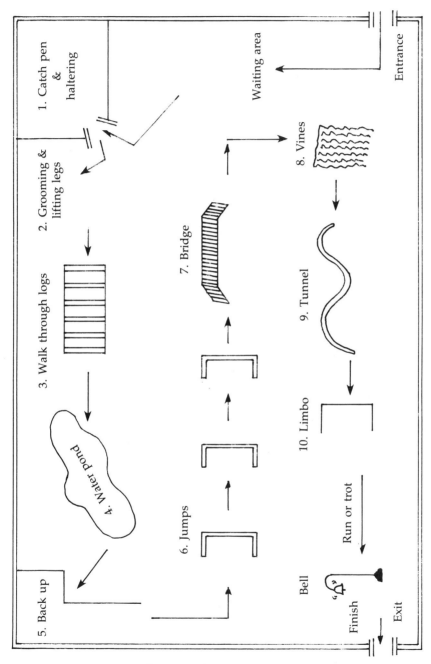

A typical pattern for an obstacle course.

"Now let's get this straight!" *Courtesy Betty Barkman.*

A llama going through the "vines" in the obstacle course.

jumps and tunnels. Sometimes designing the course is as challenging as going through it.

Before entering the ring, carefully study the diagram of the course displayed near the entrance. The judge evaluates each llama and handler as a team, while they complete the course. Sometimes there are two judges, each observing half of the course. Judges look for an enthusiastic llama that appears eager to follow his handler. Try to work with a loose lead. The event isn't timed, so there is no rush to complete the course. Walk as you would on the trail — relaxed but with a purpose. When you maneuver an obstacle unfamiliar to your llama, don't rush him; let him look it over, give him some slack, and gently encourage him to follow you.

You are given three chances to work through each obstacle. If your llama refuses to cross over any obstacle, try again. If he refuses after the third time, simply go around and on to the next one.

Pack Courses and Races — The packer's obstacle course is similar to the regular obstacle pattern, but the degree of difficulty is greater. The jumps are higher, the tunnels may require the llama to crawl, and the challenges are more exciting. This event is definitely for the more experienced handler and packer. Pack races are a real crowd pleaser. They are usually timed.

In the flapjack race, entrants put packs on their llamas, race with them to a designated position where they build a fire, prepare flapjacks, and race back to the starting point.

Another fun event is the egg and spoon race. The handler has to complete the course, leading his llama over obstacles while carrying a raw egg in a spoon! If you drop the egg, you're out. Those completing the course with an intact egg vie for the shortest time.

The PR Class (for Public Relations Llamas) — Many times llamas are asked to be ambassadors of good will. Owners take llamas to school to help educate students about the species, convalescent hospitals to cheer and entertain, or parades. These ambassador llamas must be exceptionally well-trained to accept loud noises, strange situations, petting, and special challenges without panic.

The class may simulate a parade route with cheering spectators on both sides who yell, scream, pop balloons, and clap loudly. The route may include stairs which the llama must climb up and down, and it may circle a barking dog. A mock classroom is usually included in which "students" rush up and pet the llama.

The judge scores the llama's reactions. If an entry spooks and decides to sail over the barriers and back to the stall, then it's back to the training corral!

The pack race is one of the most exciting events.

Winding through the "tunnel."

Paul Barkman with Bubba, a llama, and Betty with an alpaca. This type of act could be entered in a freestyle event.

The costume class.

Driving Classes — Entrants may be asked to pull a pony cart at different gaits, back up, and traverse various obstacles. A well-trained driving llama is calm but alert to the vocal commands and rein pressure of the handler. Driving training requires much effort.

Freestyle Classes — A llama with a unique talent may be entered into a free-style class where he has five minutes to show off. I've seen everything from llamas rolling over to smoking carrot cigarettes. One show featured a young handler preparing her llama to go to school. The llama allowed her to brush his teeth! Another llama crawled!

Costume Classes — Even though costume events are considered to be performance classes, they are not held during that part of the show. You'll see all sorts of regalia on the inaugural day of a show. Many fairs ask competitors to parade around the fairgrounds. Owners go to a lot of work, preparing costumes and training llamas to carry out their roles. The llamas patiently submit to their owners' whims, proving that they are truly unique. So pack up the gear, get out the brush, join in and plan to have fun!

CHAPTER ELEVEN

BREEDING

For anyone considering breeding llamas, the bottom line must be to improve, not merely perpetuate, the species. Quality is therefore the ultimate goal. One of a breeder's greatest rewards is to see a beautiful newborn cria that is the product of careful research and the subsequent pairing of an excellent sire and dam.

Quality encompasses conformation, soundness and temperament. Wool quality and quantity may also be a goal, but other qualities should not be sacrificed to obtain the best wool. Some breeders try to breed for a particular wool coloration, but unless you are an avid student of Mendel, this may be a hit and miss game.

I hope that the llama industry will make every effort to avoid the trap of breeding for the trendy or "typey" look. Fads such as wooly ears, smaller-sized llamas, or small, delicate heads come and go because of our notion of how we would like our llamas to look. But nature has designed the llama well. Over centuries, they have evolved into sturdy, agile animals well-equipped to traverse rough terrain with heavy loads, to flee predators, and to readily adapt as friends to man.

One sector among llama afficionado wants to see a heavily wooled face, body and legs. These animals are definitely personable, as well as supplying a great deal of fleece. Then you have the other group that wants an athletic, large, heavy-boned llama with less wool that can carry large loads on the trail. Breeders have been trying to combine all of these traits into a "super-llama." However, you can't have heavy wool on a pack animal.

If the llama industry is to have a future, perhaps it must respond to the market and breed two kinds of llamas. Purists may have to accept that the market for wool exists, and that some breeders will have no qualms about introducing alpaca in their bloodlines. The pure llama may also be perpetuated for those who desire the companion on the trail and to continue the refinement of the llama as a specific breed.

Dr. Doolittle, one of the most prolific herd sires in the U.S.
Photo courtesy of Dick and Kay Patterson, Patterson Ranch.

Thus, when planning your breeding program, analyze your objectives. Try to picture the perfect llama, and study the prospective parents. Just because the sire is a grand champion doesn't mean that he will produce the same qualities; you must study the dam also. Learn about dominant and recessive genes; some characteristics are dominant or stronger and will carry over in the offspring, thereby overriding the recessive genes. However, when recessive genes are paired with similar recessive genes, the recessive characteristics will be expressed. For example, breeding a blue-eyed male with a blue-eyed female llama will more likely result in a blue-eyed cria, as blue eyes are a recessive trait. Since most characteristics are inherited, the breeder needs to scrutinize the parents and the grandparents if possible.

LEGENDARY LLAMAS

According to the International Llama Registry, as of July 1989 the most prolific sires were Dr. Doolittle with 308 progeny, Chief Sitting Bull, 249; Errol Flynn, 230; Eclipse-PL, 227; Zorro PL, 200; Poncho

Via, 199; Fortunato, 146; The Great Gildersleeve, 127, Monsieur, 96; and Macho Camacho, 80.

Eclipse and Monsieur are both sons of Dr. Doolittle, and among them have sired over 3% of the 24,000 llamas registered with the ILR as of March 1990.

Six distinct lines are represented by these ten. Parentage of The Great Gildersleeve and Errol Flynn is unknown, as well Macho Camacho, a Chilean import. Seven of these legendary ten spent their careers at the Patterson Ranch in Sisters, Oregon.

These llamas are the grandaddies of the llama industry, and were known for their excellent conformation and fine quality of wool. Some of them are alive today, still producing outstanding crias. Many new names appearing on the horizon are routinely featured in the various breed magazines. If breeding is your goal, subscribe to all of the periodicals available to stay abreast of the market.

NEW BLOOD

Many breeders are trying to resolve the problem of a small gene pool with llamas imported from South America. But this may not be a panacea; in South America owners commonly run one male with several females for one week, exchanging him for another male the following week, and so on to be sure their females are bred. There is no way to ascertain the paternity of the crias; thus when the new females are bred for the first time two years later, they could be paired with siblings. These breeders do not keep track of bloodlines, and as South American breeders are culling their herds, in our zeal to purchase stock for outcrossing we may be importing substandard stock.

Perhaps breeders should not put such an emphasis on using well-known studs over and over again, or rely on importation, but rather look for potential in young or lesser known herd sires to bring in improved type. Yet, by outbreeding (mating individuals from populations that are geographically separate, such as Chileans and Bolivian imports), we do increase genetic diversity and, potentially, overall quality of the offspring.

UNDESIRABLE TRAITS

There are many hereditary or congenital defects that all breeders should be aware of. A hereditary defect is one that is passed on from

Oko Castizo. *Photo by M. J. Wickham, courtesy of Jim and Beula Williams, Big Trees Llama Farm.*

generation to generation; a congenital defect is present at birth, but may not necessarily be passed on to progeny.

Whether or not certain defects can be passed on is a subject of controversy within the industry. In general, most veterinarians and breeders agree that the following list of less desirable characteristics are genetic, and therefore should be kept out of your breeding stock as much as possible. Keep in mind that both the nature and magnitude of the defect, and how much it affects or impairs the animal, also play important roles. For example, if a female has short stubby ears (without loss of hearing), she could be used in your breeding program. However, if she has a producing history of choanal atresia in her young (crias that cannot nurse), she should not be bred again. She may be spayed and lead a productive life as a companion llama.

Angular Limb Deformity: Excessive and abnormal curvature of the bones and joints of the front and rear legs.

Choanal Atresia: A malformation in the nasal area making it impossible for the newborn to nurse.

The Fiduciary, a well known herd sire owned by Taylor Llamas. *Photo by Paul Taylor.*

Cow Hocks: As viewed from behind, the hocks turn in almost to the point of touching.

Dropped Fetlocks or Pasterns: A weak pastern or less than normal angle of the pastern possibly resulting in the pastern or fetlock touching the ground. (Don't panic at this problem in a newborn, as it may be a sign of prematurity and often corrects itself.)

Ectopic Testicles: One or both testicles not found in their usual location, below the rectum between the rear legs. In some cases either one or both testicles do not descend during the normal growth pattern.

Female External Genitalia Abnormalities: These include vaginal "shelving" (vulvar lips approach horizontal plane instead of normal, near-vertical plane), a tilted vulvar tip, very small vulva, or prominent clitoris (consistent with hermaphroditism).

Gopher Ears: Short, stubby ears that are not due to frostbite.

Gonadal Hypoplasia: Abnormally small testicle.

Humped Back: An increased convexity or upward curvature of the top-line of the back.

Jaw Malocclusions: Either the upper jaw is too short or the lower jaw is too long, resulting in protruding lower teeth. Occasionally the lower jaw is too short or the upper jaw is too long.

Post-Leg: Straight line from stifle to fetlock instead of normal, zig-zag configuration of hind leg when seen from the side. When viewed from the side the rear leg appears almost straight.

Sickle Hocks: Marked hock flexion causing angular rather than vertical hind cannon bone when viewed from the side. When viewed from the side the lower leg resembles the lower part of a sickle.

Sway Back: Concavity or downward curvature of the top-line.

Umbilical Hernia: Soft, fluctuant bulge at the umbilicus.

This list covers basic, major problems. Other congenital defects affect reproductive and digestive systems; if you suspect that these are occurring in your herd, consult your veterinarian immediately. Technical source books for troubleshooting such difficulties are listed in Appendix C.

Imagine the dilemma one faces in owning an outstandingly well conformed male with only one testicle. It's difficult to remove such an animal from one's breeding program, but the "buck" has to stop somewhere. No one needs to be reminded about what has happened in both pedigreed dog and horse industries when greedy, unethical breeders have ignored congenital defects.

Such llamas are simply gelded or spayed, and put to recreational or utilitarian use.

It takes at least three generations to breed out undesirable traits. In responsible culling, female llamas with minor defects can be bred to males who do not have the same or similar defects. For example, a female with particularly long, thin legs may be bred to a male with heavier, stocky bone.

Since a particular female produces only ten to fifteen crias in her lifetime, it is easier to control the quality of her offspring by choosing a sire with excellent traits. Any breeding male, on the other hand, should be as free as possible from all defects, as he has the potential to propagate hundreds of crias.

If you do plan to try to produce grand champions, breed the best to the best. Many a breeder has lamented the fact that llama owners

Eclipse, one of the leading herd sires in the U.S. owned by the Patterson Ranch. *Photo by Johnny Johnston.*

have brought their worst stock to his champion sire and then complained that the cria didn't measure up to their expectations.

THE MATING GAME

Pedigrees and Breeding Programs

Some terms breeders use include "linebreeding," "inbreeding" "cross," "outside" or "outcrossing." Linebreeding is the practice of pairing males and females that evolve from the same bloodline or ancestor. Inbreeding is the mating of more closely related animals, such as father to daughter, sibling to sibling. Cross or outside breeding refers to the coupling of totally unrelated pairs.

During the first half of this century, there were few llamas to select from and the gene pool was small. Many llamas in zoos were inbred, and small private herds were commonly linebred. In many instances, linebreeding was deliberate in order to continue or fix a particularly desirable characteristic in the offspring. Unfortunately, negative traits are propitiated as well. Know your genetics, for in the attempt to match dominant genes, you are likely to match recessive ones too.

Fortunately modern breeders are aware of the consequences of inbreeding and linebreeding and are learning all they can about genetics by taking classes, consulting researchers and discussing the issue with their veterinarian. Crossbreeding is the preferred choice; however, since most llamas are the direct descendants of a few well-known herd sires, the limited gene pool makes outcrossing difficult.

Breeding Age

We feel that females should be bred at "two or two hundred": two years or two hundred pounds, whichever occurs first, but some begin breeding them at one year of age. Since the female grows rapidly between the ages of one and two, I feel it robs her of development to breed her at the earlier age.

Males are used for stud when slightly older than females. Male llamas about a year of age have been known to impregnate females, but it is not the norm. In Peru males aren't bred until they are two-and-one-half or three years old. Since we have better nutrition in this country, our males mature earlier; thus most have viable sperm and we can begin standing them at two years.

A breeding male should have sufficient weight to force an unwilling female into a kushing position in order to breed, although many females will kush without force.

A newborn male llama's penis is completely attached to the prepuce, and his testicles are difficult to detect. At six months, you should be able to see the testicles in the scrotum. At one year, the penis begins to separate from the prepuce, and the young male will begin to take interest in the females; up to this point he will have been indiscriminate in his play, briefly mounting young males, females and even his dam. All of the play acting is preparation. The young male will nibble on his target's legs trying to get her to kush or sit so that he can mount. Young males around two years of age will learn mating behavior if allowed to observe from a distance.

Hand vs. Pasture-Breeding

Llama ranchers are divided in their opinions over "pasture-breeding" and "hand-breeding." In pasture breeding, the sire runs continually with the open female for a month or two until she appears unreceptive and spits off the male. It is very difficult to pinpoint the exact date of the successful breeding when using this approach. Some breeders rotate sires with their herds, believing that this results in a higher

Don gives a helping hand at a breeding.

conception rate. Some breeders prefer having a male in with their females for protection and social structuring.

Hand-breeding allows much more control; the male is confined with the female only for the purpose of mating. Afterwards he is removed for twelve to twenty-four hours and introduced again. Sexual libido is heightened by this method, as the male has been kept away from the female, teased by being able to see her, and has plenty of energy and interest once they are introduced. We hand-breed weekly or until the female spits off the male.

This method results in greater accuracy in pinpointing actual breeding dates, observance of penetration, and avoidance of injury to the male.

Blood Typing

In the late seventies, llamas were still relatively new in North America and some owners followed the breeding practices of South American alpaca breeders. The animals were pasture-bred, where the females are kept in one large pasture with one or two males all the time. In these particular instances, two males were kept in the herd. The owners felt that conception rates were higher due to the competition factor. The males were more aggressive in their mating behavior, and some males seemed to prefer certain females while leaving others open.

Unfortunately, this caused confusion as to the true parentage of the offspring. Which male was the sire? Pasture breeding has been common in the cattle and horse industries. In order to verify parentage in those groups, blood typing has been utilized since 1920. Just recently, basic studies of blood group factors have been carried out in llamas. To date, the major source of research has been conducted at the serology laboratory at the University of California, Davis.

Blood typing consists of taking blood samples from the cria, dam and all possible sires. Through a process of matching and elimination, the researcher can eliminate potential sires and therefore leave you with the most likely sire. Blood typing does not point out the sire but eliminates any that does not qualify. So for the owner who has pasture-bred or who has had males "jump the fence," the doubt of parentage has also been eliminated.

If you are planning on breeding on your own ranch and are thinking of purchasing a herd sire, request that the owner have the male blood typed. The cost is around $30 for U.C. Davis plus the veterinarian's charge to draw blood and forward the sample to the University. For the peace of mind, the expense is minimal. If at all possible, all breeding stock, male or female should be blood typed.

At the present time, many llama owners are suggesting that the International Llama Registry require blood typing as a prerequisite to registration. Many cattle and horse registries have already adopted this procedure.

Ovulation and Estrus

Unlike many mammals that have heats or seasons, llamas are induced ovulators; this means that the egg is released *after* mating takes place. To understand this induced ovulation or anovulatory estrus, you need to know some of the basic physiology of the female llama. Like most mammals, the llama has a uterus, cervix and ovaries. The ovaries are positioned at the tips of the uterine horns. Each ovary takes turns in what is termed as constant follicular waves. As the follicle on one ovary matures, the female is more receptive to the male. If copulation takes place, the follicle will continue to mature, and ovulation occurs. If there is no mating or stimulus, the follicle will be reabsorbed, and the follicle on the other ovary will mature in the next wave. Mating must take place in order to stimulate ovulation.

The female will be more receptive to the male on some days than on others; she will assume a kushing position or sit down immediately

Inquisitive!

for the male. When this takes place, we assume that she is in the peak of one of the waves. Since the follicles are mature for a period of ten to twelve days and it takes three to five days for the next one to mature, there is a good chance that you can catch her at a peak time with repeated breedings.

Once fertilization has taken place, progesterone increases and may be measured in blood samples. To verify pregnancy, have your veterinarian draw a blood sample thirty days after mating. The results of this progesterone level test takes three to four days.

Breeding Schedules

Gestation is approximately eleven-and-one-half months or from 340 to 360 days. To avoid the arrival of crias in the hottest summer months or in the worst winter months, mate accordingly. Most breeders prefer the fall and spring, thus avoiding both heat stress and hypothermia. We try to breed so crias arrive in pairs; they are better socialized when two or more grow and play together.

Breeding Records of Sire

DATE OF BIRTH _____
****

DATE:_____ DAM _____TOTAL TIME:_____

DAM'S OWNER AND ADDRESS:_____

REMARKS:_____

RE-BREEDING DATE_____TOTAL TIME:_____COMMENTS_____

RE-BREEDING DATE_____TOTAL TIME:_____COMMENTS_____

PREGNANCY TEST DATE:_____RESULTS:_____2ND TEST DATE:_____RESULTS____

CRIA BIRTH DATE:_____CRIA NAME:_____

SEX:_____WEIGHT:_____TIME:_____COMMENTS_____

****

DATE:_____ DAM _____TOTAL TIME:_____

DAM'S OWNER AND ADDRESS:_____

REMARKS:_____

RE-BREEDING DATE_____TOTAL TIME:_____COMMENTS_____

RE-BREEDING DATE_____TOTAL TIME:_____COMMENTS_____

PREGNANCY TEST DATE:_____RESULTS:_____2ND TEST DATE:_____RESULTS____

CRIA BIRTH DATE:_____CRIA NAME:_____

SEX:_____WEIGHT:_____TIME:_____COMMENTS_____

****

DATE:_____ DAM _____TOTAL TIME_____

DAM'S OWNER AND ADDRESS:_____

REMARKS:_____

RE-BREEDING DATE:_____TOTAL TIME:_____COMMENTS_____

RE-BREEDING DATE:_____TOTAL TIME:_____COMMENTS_____

PREGNANCY TEST DATE:_____RESULTS:_____2ND TEST DATE:_____RESULTS:____

CRIA BIRTH DATE:_____CRIA NAME:_____

SEX:_____WEIGHT:_____TIME:_____COMMENTS:_____

****

Pay particular attention to the time that you first breed, as you are setting the pattern for future breedings. Your schedule can repeat year after year, since you normally breed a female back two to three weeks after parturition.

Most llamas are receptive in early morning and evening. We breed for the first time in the morning, the second that same evening and a third time the following morning. We record dates and times as well as any information we feel may be pertinent. Log this information and keep it with your files.

After the first three breedings on days one and two, we wait one week and repeat three consecutive breedings on days seven and eight if the female is receptive. Again we wait one week and breed again. We repeat this schedule until the female spits off the male and refuses to sit down for him. In some cases, the female will spit off the male by the second week. In other instances, the female will allow a highly aggressive male to breed her even after fertilization has taken place. In most cases, the female will spit the male off after two weeks. We then wait for thirty days and draw blood for a progesterone test. If it is positive, ninety days later we test again to make sure she has retained the fetus and the pregnancy is progressing normally.

Llamas have a 30% tendency to abort in the first ninety days, or if the fetus is small enough it may be reabsorbed into the mother's system. It may seem expensive to keep testing, but you avoid waiting an entire year for a cria that never arrives.

Periodically we walk our male through the females' pen. When he returns with a little bit of "green" from everyone, then we're satisfied for another month.

Males can often tell first who is pregnant and who isn't. If a particular llama is pregnant, she'll point her nose in the air and make clucking sounds. If the male persists and tries to mount or nibble at her legs to get her to kush, she'll reward him with a well-placed bolus of spit. After a few of these, he proceeds to the next female who will hopefully react the same way. However, if a female kushes and is receptive, he is immediately returned to his pen (unless he is the intended sire), and we proceed to re-breed her.

In the case of the seasoned female llama, we breed back one week from parturition. Some breeders wait two weeks, while others wait one month. We have chosen the one-week term, as it has produced the greatest number of pregnancy-positive breedings.

Don't breed back this early if the dam has had a difficult birth such as a retained placenta, expulsion of the uterus, torn uterus, or other complications. In such instances, follow your veterinarian's advice.

This herd sire knows there is an open female nearby. In a fantasy world known only to the llama, he throws his head back and contemplates the conquest.

Sometimes the girls need a little coaxing.

The male orgles, while the female sits placidly.

"Success, even if we have to put up with this little guy. I just wish he wouldn't take so many notes!"

If your dam has had any unusual discharge from the vulva such as pink mucous in excess of approximately two tablespoons, have her checked. She may have an infection, and you will put her at risk if you attempt to breed back.

If possible, designate one area for hand-breeding your llamas; your herd sire will recognize it as his area to perform. An area 30'x 30' will suffice. The terrain should be fairly level.

Getting Down to Business

Have your veterinarian examine the female before you breed to insure that there are no obvious problems such as an intact hymen. She should be current on shots and worming. If you take her to another ranch, the sire's owner may require that you have a current health certificate and vet check, especially if he guarantees a live cria. Visiting males or females should be isolated from the main herd.

Also have your veterinarian check your male before breeding him the first time. The male's fighting teeth should be removed before you breed him. The male nibbles on the female's ears during courtship, and could tear her ears if she is uncooperative.

If you are breeding a maiden llama it's best to use an older, experienced male since they tend to be more tolerant. Likewise, if you are using a young male for the first time, it's best to use an experienced female. Two novices can frustrate one another. You may want to keep your male haltered for easy handling.

Try to keep the main herd away from the activity, although an experienced male will not be distracted if a hundred people were present. However, a young stud will often visit with the other females along the fence line and have to be reminded of his duty.

Take the female into the breeding area and cross-tie her. Have your assistant hold the halter and talk to her reassuringly. Trim excess wool away from the tail area and back of the rump with scissors or shears. If she has a young cria, make sure it is nearby and visible through a fence. Don't leave the cria in the breeding pen.

Using a good grade of vet wrap that can be purchased at any feed store, start at the base of the tail and wrap the material around the tail in a circular motion, working towards the tip. The wrap will adhere to itself and not to the wool.

Remove the females lead rope and let her wander around the breeding pen while you bring the sire. Introduce him with his halter on and then stand back. The male will go up to the female and sniff her. He may or may not attempt to mount right away. She will usually prance away, and he will chase her. When she stops and digs her feet in, he will try to mount her again and force her down. If she continues to resist, he will nibble on her front legs, making her tuck them under.

Sometimes some romancing is necessary and it may take awhile for the male to display interest, or he may take one look at the female, and dash off to hide in the barn. Be patient and don't panic; you may have to pair your llamas up for several days in a row before they accomplish their task.

The penis resembles a long curling worm and turns in a corkscrew motion when it searches for the vulva. Once it has found its target the male will readjust his position, moving more closely to and tightly against the female. The hocks will be lined up and be very close to each other. Notice the proper positioning in the accompanying photos.

Once the male successfully forces the female to sit and appears to be in position, we go to his side to help line the penis up with the vulva. Don't be afraid to observe closely if you have to, or to lift up his wool. Both llamas will be preoccupied.

When working with very wooly llamas, it may be impossible to observe them from the side. In these instances, I approach the male llama from the rear and run my hand below his testicles and along the penal shaft. If my fingers can follow the shaft to the tip of the vulva, then I know he has penetrated. This may take practice, but will reassure you that he is making contact.

On occasion your female llama will lie on her side. Try to reposition her; if you can't, let the breeding continue.

As the male begins to copulate, he orgles. Unlike other familiar sounds that llamas make, this occurs only during breeding. Copulation can take from five to forty-five minutes. The male emits semen in a steady dribble rather than in spurts, and may climb off and on the female several times.

When he is finished, he will retreat to a corner to rest. At this time you should check the female. You will see semen in and around the vulva. Don't be alarmed if you see some blood, especially likely with maiden llamas. Remove the tail wrap before returning the female to the herd, and replace it before the next breeding.

CHAPTER TWELVE

BIRTHING

When we began raising llamas, we were lucky enough to see one of our dams give birth for the first time. It was several years before we were able to see another one; no matter how much time I spent in the barn, my female llamas decided to have their crias when I went to the store. My discussion with other breeders reveals this to be a common phenomenon. At first we thought that the dams didn't want us around for their big moment, but in reality, while there are several signs to watch for, llamas don't loudly indicate that birth is imminent.

Thirty days before the targeted due date, move the pregnant llama to her "maternity suite," where you can observe her easily. Keep her stall clean, and make sure the birthing supplies are on hand.

The dam should be up to date on her vaccinations and may be wormed with a paste wormer. Be sure to consult your veterinarian in these matters. He may want to give a booster of all vaccinations in addition to an injection of selenium to protect your cria against White Muscle Disease. Trim the wool around the females hindquarters, but not on the tail.

BIRTHING SUPPLIES

Prepare a birthing kit of items to use in treating the dam and cria. A list of the equipment to keep on hand appears below:

Heater (safe type, purchased from feed store or livestock equipment dealer.)
Scales
Clean towels
Thermometer
Iodine (7%)
Betadine
Small plastic cup

Child's nasal syringe
Child's Fleet enema
Scissors
Dental floss
Small bowl for washing hands
Medication recommended by your vet

You may never need to use some of these items, but they're essential in an emergency. You need towels to dry off the cria. If you have to tie the umbilical cord off, dental floss or string will suffice. You can use a nasal syringe to suction mucous, and a thermometer to check the cria's temperature.

Sometimes the newborn llama has difficulty passing his first feces (meconium), and it is helpful to have some *Pet* enemas on hand. Mild soapy water in a syringe will also work well in an emergency.

Make a list of birthing procedures, and place it with the supplies. Go over the list with your family or assistants; you may want to have them read over this chapter to understand what they need to do in the event that you are unavailable.

THE BIRTH PROCESS

Labor

Regrettably, your llama will not hang a sign out the window that reads, "Today is the day!". Some female llamas give no warning. You can interpret some signals, however.

If you have carefully observed your llama, you will be familiar with her various habits and demeanor. Watch for anything that isn't the norm for her. On the other hand, llamas are individuals; if you don't observe these signs, don't panic.

Two to four weeks before delivery, the udder may swell and in some cases turn bright pink. Wax that looks like small tear drops forms on the teats. A milk vein that runs along the stomach will protrude slightly.

Your llama may roll more often in the dust pile, and may lie in the kush position with her rear legs stretched out to the side. She may moan or hum more often. Our llama Domino begins a steady hum a day before she gives birth. Your prospective mother may not be hungry, but will drink her usual amount of water. But I find this the least likely sign, as one of our llamas eats during delivery.

Within one to twenty-four hours before birth, you may see discharge around the vulva, and your llama may get up and down constantly or pace the fence. But for us, by far the most tried and true signal has been when the dam begins to isolate from other females in our birthing area and refuses to go into the stall. When a normally gregarious llama becomes a loner, we are nearly certain that she will have her cria the next day.

Delivery

Llamas commonly give birth in the morning to midday. As the moment approaches, she may assume various positions from standing to lying down. Try to keep her away from walls or fences, as she may swing around and injure the cria in her attempt to deliver it. Resist the temptation to rush in and assist; unless there are difficulties, let nature run its course.

The cria is encased in the placenta, a blue-tinged, transparent sac of membranes. When the sac starts to emerge, you may see a nose inside or there may be one or two feet. If you only see one foot right away, don't panic; as birth progresses, both feet should join the nose or vice versa. Normally the sac will break on its own as the cria is pushed through the vagina. If the bag is still intact once head and feet are out, break it with your fingers. A slight tug will suffice.

The cria will sputter, gasp, cough and shake his head as he dangles from the vagina. Again, don't panic; the more he does this the better. He is clearing his airways of amniotic fluid.

Your cria's feet may appear below or above the head and appear to hang there for some time. You may even imagine that he will strangle from the tight opening. Gradually, more of the legs and neck will appear; then there will seem to be an endless wait until his shoulders pass through. Your dam will bear down hard, as this is the largest part of the offspring to deliver. If the shoulders seem to be bound for over ten minutes, slightly rotate the body forty-five degrees to the left or right. If you are unfamiliar with this technique, have your veterinarian demonstrate it to you before your llama goes into labor.

Once the cria's shoulders are through, the rest of delivery should take place quickly. If this process seems long, consider that the average time for parturition is around twenty minutes; but I have had some deliveries take as long as forty-five.

If you see only one leg and no nose, or any other position that seems unusual, call your vet immediately, as the cria may have to be turned. Fortunately, birthing difficulties are rare.

Here the tip of one foot is starting to emerge. Sometimes you may see the nose first.

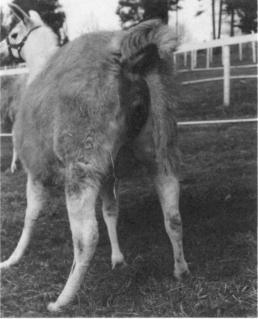

Soon one foot starts to emerge. (Sometimes you will see the nose first.)

As the dam bears down you may see feces being pushed out. Here the
cria's foot and nose are starting to emerge. They may recede
and emerge again several times.

"Who's there?"
Lucena relaxes a bit.
The cria's legs are
now prominent.

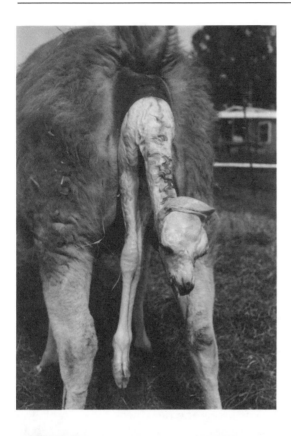

Let the cria hang down so the fluids can drain out of the airways.

It's over. The dam takes a breather while the herd admires the new baby.

Most llamas give birth in a standing position. Owners are sometimes concerned that the cria will be injured falling to the ground, and attempt to catch him. But there are reasons to let the cria fall. First, the umbilical cord is being stretched and the blood vessels squeezed off; thus, when the cord breaks, bleeding is minimal. Second, the sudden shock of hitting the ground helps stimulate the cria's nervous system and oxygen intake.

If your dam is cooperative and lets you near the cria, rub him briskly with clean towels to stimulate and dry him off quickly. Unlike other mammals, mother llamas do not clean or lick their offspring; it is especially important that he is dried and warmed quickly in bad weather.

Postpartum Care

Take the cria's temperature, gently inserting the thermometer no more than two inches into his rectum. His temperature may vary slightly but should be around 101° F. If it is below 100° F, warm him by placing him on a heating pad or using a hair dryer set on warm (not hot). You may need to place a heater in the stall.

Put your finger in the cria's mouth to check if his lower incisors have erupted; if not, he may be premature. Also check for mucous and to be sure he has a good sucking reflex.

Dip the cria's umbilical cord in iodine; if it's longer than four inches, cut it to that length. You may wish to tie it off at four inches with dental floss, making your cut below the tie. Check for an umbilical hernia (a bulge of tissue at the navel). If the hernia is small, it may shrink by itself; if it's larger, consult your veterinarian.

Check your new llama's sex, and weigh him so that you can keep accurate growth and nutrition records. A hanging scale that weighs up to fifty pounds works well. We gently restrain our struggling new cria in a duffle bag, hanging the bag on the scales with his head free or tucked inside. Normal newborns weigh from twenty to thirty-five pounds; any cria under twenty pounds may be premature and needs careful observation to make sure he is strong enough to nurse. Don't worry if he doesn't gain the first day, but after that his average weight gain should be at least ¼ pound per day, the more the better.

We use a chart to record birth information on both cria and dam. If a birth was atypical, this material is useful in taking precautions the following year. Keeping the weight chart helps monitor the cria's growth rate.

Don weighs the cria
in a duffle bag.

Postpartum Care of the Dam

Let your cria rest while you attend to his mother. Halter her, and
have your assistant hold her gently against a wall. Wash your hands
with *Betadine* and wipe her udder with a clean rag soaked in the same
solution. This helps prevent infection of the teats and udder (mastitis).
Rinse well. Gently pull on each teat, removing wax as necessary and
drawing down the colostrum. Rub some colostrum over the bag so
the cria will smell it; he will resist nursing if he can smell the *Betadine*.

If the cria is small and weak, place him under his mother and put
his mouth right on a teat; this seems to speed things up and insure
our peace of mind. If the llama resists your aid, stand back and let
her offspring figure out how to nurse on his own. If the cria gets up
within forty-five minutes and seems active, leave the pair alone.

First Milk

First milk or colostrum is thick, yellow, and contains the antibodies needed to insure the newborn cria's immunity. When the cria is first born, his rumen tolerates colostrum, but after twenty-four hours, according to most research, he will have obtained its maximum benefits.

Some breeders keep goat colostrum on hand for dams that refuse to nurse or that lack milk. Keep it in a freezer (not a frost-free one, as this appliance will defrost and freeze again, destroying the antibodies in the colostrum). In optimum conditions, frozen colostrum keeps for seven years. After twenty-four hours, or if your dam is still unable or unwilling to nurse, a recommended supplement or surplus from another nursing dam should be given. A word of caution — when heating colostrum to give to the newborn, *never* use the microwave. The valuable anti-bodies will be destroyed.

Plasma Transfer

If a cria hasn't nursed within the first twelve hours, or if we know that the dam is short on milk from previous experience, we take both dam and newborn to our veterinarian, who transfuses the cria with blood plasma from the dam. This will give him excellent immunity. Twenty-four hours after the transfusion, we have blood drawn from the cria again to check the immunoglobulin level.

Delivery of the Placenta

Watch for the delivery of the placenta or afterbirth within three to six hours of the birth. It will look like a large blue ball as it is expelled from the vagina. Take it outside and spread it on the ground to make sure it is whole (see photo). If it is torn, pieces may have remained in the uterus, which could cause infection. If you are in doubt about this, consult your veterinarian. While some vaginal discharge after birth is normal, if it persists, remember not to rebreed and to seek professional advice.

Bonding

Most llamas are excellent mothers with plenty of milk, attentive to and protective of their offspring. But a first-time dam may be confused about her duties. Despite your overwhelming desire to play midwife to Mother Nature, make every effort to leave the two alone together to work things out. If your dam is overweight, check her teats and udder for milk before you leave the pair alone.

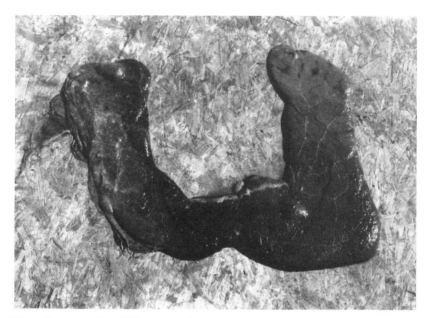

The placenta should be spread out and inspected to make sure it is whole. A partially retained placenta will cause uterine infection.

Watch them from a distance. Steel yourself against the spraddling falls your cria will take as he tries to make his way around. He will nurse at the stall boards, his mother's legs, and anything else he finds until he hits the jackpot. When he finds the udder and discovers a teat, he will suckle joyously and loudly. His first meal will only be a few minutes long as he switches from one teat to the other. Rest assured that he is getting a good drink of colostrum, and will need a short nap.

Keep dam and newborn indoors for the first day to promote bonding and monitor milk intake. After that, if the weather is moderate or warm, turn them out. Your herd will swarm around the newcomer, humming as if commenting on the dam's accomplishment. "Mickie," one of our females, is always hysterical to watch when her crias make their debut. She struts around the birthing area with head high and tail up and circles the cria, proudly clucking and clicking. This activity continues for a half hour until the curious crowd gets bored and dissipates.

Some breeders prefer to leave birthing to Mother Nature and allow their llamas to give birth in the herd. However, the mortality rate in

The cria may have difficulty locating his lunch.

Mom will usually help out by nuzzling him around the tail.

This cria is twenty minutes old.

The same female two hours later.

Cria Birth Record

CRIA NAME_____

NAME OF SIRE_____NAME OF DAM_____

COMMENTS ON DAMS LABOR_____

DATE OF BIRTH:_____TIME:_____A.M.__P.M.___

BODY TEMPERATURE_____° BIRTH WEIGHT_____

SEX_____ WAS UMBILICAL CORD TREATED?_____TYPE?_____

ANY UMBILICAL HERNIA PRESENT?_____ENEMA GIVEN?_____

ANY ABNORMALITIES PRESENT? IF SO, DESCRIBE:_____

_____

TIME FIRST NURSING OBSERVED:_____WAS COLOSTRUM GIVEN?_____

TYPE_____ AMOUNT_____

TIME PLACENTA WAS PASSED:_____WAS PLACENTA WHOLE?_____

ANY UNUSUAL DISCHARGE FROM THE DAM?_____

ATTENDING VETERINARIAN_____

MEDICATION OR TREATMENT GIVEN:_____

WEIGHT/TEMPERATURE CHART

DATE	TIME	TEMP.	WEIGHT	DATE	TIME	TEMP.	WEIGHT

Keep good birthing records. Here is an example of a form
the author uses.

Peru for newborn llamas in the first three days is fifty percent. The steep hillsides in that country cause newborns to roll far away from their dams, and tall grasses make it hard for them to nurse; without early nourishment, they deteriorate rapidly in the cold nights. In the U.S., loss of crias is approximately five percent.

PREMATURE CRIAS

Symptoms of prematurity include tipped ears that seem to bend in half, low birth weight, walking on the pasterns (the cria appears to walk on his heels) and general lethargy.

If the cria seems to droop and hangs over the dung pile with no results, try giving him a *Pet* enema or use a mild soap solution. Within minutes, he will pass a thick black plug of first stool. A healthy cria will generally do this on his own. He'll perk up immediately. Some breeders give the enema as a matter of course. Consult your veterinarian for the most appropriate way to care for the premature cria.

Hand-Feeding

In most instances, the dam will have some milk, so your function is only to supplement. The following procedures apply to the orphan cria or a dam that fails to lactate.

We have successfully fed Land o' Lakes *Lamb Lac* mixed one cup of powder to two cups of water. To this we add one cup of liquid low fat milk. It isn't necessary to sterilize either the utensils or the water used in the formula.

Lamb nipples are available from your local feed store. Use them on glass soft drink bottles or thoroughly cleansed plastic bottles. Plan to feed every four hours for the first two weeks, then increase amount and time between feedings. Weigh your cria daily.

Although it would be convenient to keep your bottle fed cria in the house, we discourage this practice, as it is important that the cria bond to its mother. As noted, male bottlefed crias may confuse their dam with their human nurturer, and can become pushy and dangerously aggressive when they mature. Through snow, rain and darkness we take turns trudging to the barn to feed with mother and herd close by.

Kneel in the stall, straddle the cria, and hug his head to your chest with the left hand. Position his neck in a "U" shape as if he were nursing from his dam. Holding the bottle with your right hand, gently force the mouth open with your fingers to push the nipple in and

This cria is underweight and weak, but alive.

Dr. Frey demonstrates the position of the ears of a weak or ill cria.

Getting a newborn to take a bottle takes patience.

This little girl finally gets the idea.

"Gosh Mom, keeping my balance is tough."

"Hey, this is a great life!"

out until he sucks. The first few attempts can be frustrating; when your cria gets the idea, he'll drink the milk down rapidly.

Start with six to eight ounces per feeding the first week and by the third week your cria should accept nearly sixteen ounces.

CRIA CARE

Mama llamas do an excellent job as mothers, making it easy for the owner. We keep a close eye on the newborns for the first thirty days, monitoring the weight gain and observing for any illness. Coughing, high fever and general lethargy merits a call to the vet. After thirty days the cria is more than likely to be on his way to healthy puberty.

Weaning

Removing the dam from the cria is usually done around five to six months after parturition. As noted before, crias can be ingenious when it comes to stealing a drink from mom. Mothers will be very accommodating standing next to the fence so the cria can squeeze that long neck between the rails. Both will be very upset about the separation, pacing the fence and moaning constantly. This lasts for four to five days, then they will resume activity with their respective herds. We wait about three months before returning a weanling female cria to her dam's herd to make sure the tie is broken and she will not try to nurse.

AFTERWORD

It is twilight, my favorite time of the day. The family awaits my presence in the kitchen but I want to enjoy a few special moments. I walk to the maternity area and on tip toes, I enter one of the stalls. A dam is kushed with her cria at her side.

Not wanting to disturb the serenity of the scene, I seek a quiet corner and settle in the warm straw. The scents of summer past surround me. There is no sound other than the humming from the mother. It sounds like a mantra, and the cria answers in his own low-pitched hum.

The cria is tired from his long day and sits snuggled against his mother. With a long sigh, he stretches out his neck and rests his head atop his mother's back. Within moments, his eyes close and his head starts to wobble from side to side. In a sudden jerk, the eyes open and he realizes he has fallen asleep. The dam looks back and nuzzles him to let him know all is okay. It is permissible to sleep.

I study her bolus as it travels up her long neck. She ruminates for a few moments and then swallows. Occasionally, she pauses to glance over at me with caution in her eye. Why should this human be in this stall? When she is satisfied that I am not a threat, the chewing continues.

I am in awe. What is the mystique? What is this attraction that draws us to the llama? Could it be that we are fascinated with the contentment, serenity and peace that seems to surround these lovely creatures? Perhaps the fast paced lives that we lead, the long lines, the demands placed on us and all the worries of mankind have something to do with it.

By sharing moments like these with our beloved animals, we too share in some of that peace.

The Triple J Herd Maintenance Feeding Program

Goals
— Birth weights above 25 pounds
— Better milk production in dams
— Balanced diet in minerals and vitamins
— Less weight fluctuation during lactation
— Finer wool quality

Pasture Separations
Group 1: Mothers with babies at their side. These llamas get 1 flake alfalfa and ½ lb. of grain per adult animal fed per day. Pasture is free choice.

Group 2: Weaned female babies to breeding (1 to 1.5 years) get ¼ lb. of grain fed once per day with 1 flake alfalfa. Free choice pasture.

Group 3: Weaned males to about 18 months get ¼ lb. grain once per day, 1 flake alfalfa per day. Free choice pasture.

Group 4: Males 18 months and older, 1 flake alfalfa, ¼ lb. grain per day. Free choice pasture.

Group 5: Bred females pregnant 1 to 9 months. These llamas get 1 flake alfalfa with ½ lb. grain in the morning. When pasture is growing, alfalfa is given at a minimum.

Group 6: Bred females 9 to 10 months to term in pergnancy get 1 flake alfalfa with ½ lb. of grain per animal fed once per day. When pasture is growing alfalfa is given at a minimum.

Group 7: Older females. These animals are pampered. Their crias are weaned at 3 to 4 months. Many times they will be kept in a pasture getting ½lb./day grain all year long. If they have lost weight during lactation we will give them one or two lbs. grain a day in individual containers to regain their weight.

Group 8: Obese females. These females can look at hay and get fat when kept in large groups. Excessive fat may impair reproduction with the possibility of increased embryonic mortality. For this reason obese females with fat on their chest and excessive roundness on their upper thighs, and legs that rub together are put in a diet pen to receive ¼ flake of alfalfa per day and ¼ lb. grain. When they achieve their proper weight, they are returned to group four and watched closely. If they start gaining weight again they are put back in the diet pen.

You should not put females on an excessive diet in their final trimester of pregnancy since this is when the fetus is getting most of its growth.

Vaccination Schedule

1. Bred females — Check with your veterinarian. You may decide to booster with CDT prior to parturition.

2. Babies at birth — 3cc Calfguard and 2cc BOSE.

3. Babies at 4 to 6 weeks — 2cc Covexin sub-cutaneous, 2cc BOSE.

4. Worming all aminals three times per year with Ivermectin alternated with Panacur and dust each time with Sevin.

Triple J Llama Mix Formula

30 lbs Dicalcium PO4	900 lbs corn	40 lbs salt
900 lbs mill run	400 lbs oats	1380 lbs barley
20 lbs permapell binder	250 lbs soybean	100 lbs molasses
50 lbs animal premix 5*		

* PREMIX 5 Guaranteed Potencies Per Pound

Vitamin A	USP Units	1,200,000	Folic Acid 14mg
Vitamin D3	USP Units	600,000	Sulphur 4.35‰
Vitamin E	USP Units	900	Potassium 3.55‰
Vitamin B12	milligrams	1.2	Magnesium 2.15‰
Riboflavin	milligrams	900	Manganese 4‰
Niacine	milligrams	3,000	Zinc 4P
d-Pantothenic Acid	milligrams	1,200	Iron 2‰
Choline	milligrams	48,000	Copper .4‰
			Iodine .12‰
			Selenium .004‰

Summary:	Grain	3rd Cutting Alfalfa
Total Protein	13.2‰	20‰
Digestible Protein	11.1‰	15.2‰
Crude Fiber	4.2‰	25‰
TDN	68.4‰	63‰
CA	.26‰	1.83‰
PO^4	1.00‰	.18‰

Llama Associations and Organizations

National/International

Alpaca Owners & Breeders Assn.
P. O. Box 1992
Estes Park, CO 80517-1992
(970) 586-5357
email: kenaoba@aol.com

Alpaca & Llama Show Assn.
P. O. Box 1189
Lyons, CO 80540
(303) 823-0659

Canadian Llama Association
#2 Notre Dame Crescent
Leduc, AB T9E 6H8

International Llama Association
2755 S. Locust St., Ste. 114
Denver, CO 80222
(303) 756-9004

International Llama Registry
P. O. Box 8
Kalispell, MT 59903
(406) 755-3438

Llama Assn. of North America
1800 S. Obenchain Road
Eagle Point, OR 97524
(541) 830-5262
llamainfo@aol.com

Natural Fiber Producers Assn.
1890 St. George Road
Danville, CA 94526
(510) 735-7804

Regional Associations

Greater Appalachian Llama Assn.
Hilary Ware
(207) 527-2319

Hoosier Llama Association
Tom Riley, Pres.
(317) 873-6626

Llama Assn. of Mid-Atlantic States
(540) 439-4665

Northern Rockies Llama Assn.
(406) 449-7093

Ohio River Valley Llama Assn.
(614) 474-2232

South Central Llama Assn.
(903) 645-2650

Southern States Llama Assn.
(704) 891-2810

State Associations

ALASKA

Alaska Chapter ILA
Larry Dreese
(907) 373-3320

CALIFORNIA

California Alpaca Breeders Assn.
9234 Champs de Elysses
Forestville, CA 95436
(707) 543-3873

California Chapter ILA
25900 Fairview Ave.
Hayward, CA 94542
(510) 583-3393

Central Coast Llama Assn.
6951 Old Adobe Cyn. Rd.
Templeton, CA 93465
(805) 466-5088

Gold Country Llama Assn.
7580 Shelborne Dr.
Granite Bay, CA 95746
(916) 791-0793

Llama Assn. of Southern California
P. O. Box 876
Norco, CA 91760

Yosemite Llama Breeders
15301 Tuolumne Rd.
Sonora, CA 95370
(209) 532-5411

Llamas of the Wine Country
P. O. Box 750518
Petaluma, CA 94975
(707) 942-9708

IDAHO

Western Idaho Llama Assn.
Jay Rais
(208) 888-4526

ILLINOIS

Illinois Llama Assn.
Scott May
(217) 935-8745

KENTUCKY

Kentucky Llama/Alpaca Assn.
Linda Huber
(606) 873-1622

MINNESOTA

Llamas of Minnesota
Pam Jensen
(608) 687-8509

MICHIGAN

Michigan Llama Assn.
Ray Howard
(616) 796-6162

MISSOURI

Missouri Llama Assn.
Deb Kell
(573) 674-4169

OREGON

Central Oregon Llama Assn.
P. O. Box 5334
Bend, OR 97708
(800) 241-LAMA

Llamas of Eastern Oregon
64153 Aspen Rd.
LaGrande, OR 97850
(503) 963-7595

Umpqua Valley Llama Assn.
P. O. Box 1805
Roseburg, OR 97470
(503) 679-6753

Willamette Valley Llama Assn.
4256 Roberts Ridge Road S.
Salem, OR 97302
(503) 581-5760

UTAH

Utah Llama Assn.
Daryl Wood
(801) 846-2525

WASHINGTON

Inland NW Llama Assn.
P. O. Box 762
Veradale, WA 99037
(509) 238-6961

Llama Owners of Washington State
3430 Pacific Ave. S. E., Ste. A-6, 317
Olympia, WA 98501
(800) 399-LAMA

Mt. Baker Llama Owners
P. O. Box 28753
Bellingham, WA 98228

Southwest Washington Llama Assn.
20719 NE 68th St.
Vancouver, WA 98682
(360) 254-1157

WISCONSIN

Wisconsin Org. of Llama Enthus.
Barb Reinecke
(920) 923-0581

Sources of Other Information

Books

Barkman, Betty and Paul, *A Well Trained Llama*. 34190 Lodge Road, Tollhouse, California 93667. $27.50 postpaid. 96 pp, many photos. Second edition by a pair who have trained everything rom elephants to reptiles.

Barkman, Betty, *Llamas in Their Formative Years*. Same address as above.

Beattie, Dr. Linda C., and Cathy Crisman, *Making the Most of Your Llama*. Kopacetic Ink, P.O. Box 1117, Longview, Washington 98632. $16.20 postpaid. A general handbook plus a section on ground driving.

Bodington, Helen, *Llama Training on Your Own: Step By Step Instructions*. Polite Pets, 697 Fawn Drive, San Anselmo, California 94960. 1986. $20.00 postpaid.

Calle Escobar, Rigoberto, *Animal Breeding and Production of American Camelids*. Lima, Peru, 1984. Available from Wordsmith, Inc., 1731-21st St., Santa Monica, California 90404. $25.00 postpaid. 358 pages with charts, sketches and photos. Translated from Spanish.

Dal Porto, Cheryl, and Francie Greth-Peto, Editors, *The Best of 3-L Llama: The First Five Years*. Llamas magazine, P.O. Box 100, Herald, California 95638. $17.75 postpaid. A selection from the 1979-1983 issues of the original *Llamas* Magazine.

Daugherty, Stanlynn, *Packing With Llamas*. Juniper Ridge Press, P.O. Box 338, Ashland, Oregon 97520. 1989. $13.95 postpaid. 210 pages, 75 photos. A must for the llama owner who wants to go backpacking.

Faiks, Jan, Jim Faiks, and Phyllis Tozier, *Llama Training: Who's In Charge?* Faik's Alpacas and Llamas, Box 521152, Big Lake, Alaska 99652. $15.00 postpaid. The first llama training manual to be published.

Fowler, Murray E. DVM, *Medicine and Surgery of South American Camelids: Llama, Alpaca, Vicuna, Guanaco*. Iowa State University Press, 2121 S. State Ave., Ames, Iowa 50010. $76.95 postpaid. This 400 page textbook and reference for veterinarians will be of interest to many llama breeders as well. Written by one of the best known llama veterinary researchers.

Freeman, Myra, *Heat Stress: Prevention, Management and Treatment in Llamas*. Sunshine States Llama Association Marketplace, Rt. 1, Box 346, Lula, Georgia 30554. $15.00 postpaid.

Hart, Rosana, *Living With Llamas: Adventures, Photos and a Practical Guide*. Juniper Ridge Press, Box 338, Ashland, Oregon 97520. Second Edition, 1987. $11.95 postpaid. 192 pages. A personal account of one couple's llama adventures plus a guide to owning and caring for llamas.

Hart, Rosana, *Llamas For Love And Money*, Juniper Ridge Press, P.O. Box 338, Ashland, Oregon 97520-0012. 272 pages. $16.95 postpaid. This is Rosana's latest book to be published in early 1991.

Hoffman, Clare, DVC, and Ingrid Asmus, *Caring For Llamas: A Health And Management Guide*. Rocky Mountain Llama Association, 168 Emerald Mountain Ct., Livermore, Colorado 80536. 1989. $20.40 postpaid. 150 pages. A must have item in every llama library.

Johnson, LaRue W., DVM, PHD, Guest Editor, *Veterinary Clinics of North America: Food Animal Practice* (Llama medicine). W.B. Saunders C., P.O. Box 6467, Duluth, Minnesota 55806-9854. Vol. 5, No. 1, March 1989. $29.00 postpaid. 236 pages. Includes articles by over a dozen contributors, mostly veterinarians and professors, on llama medicine.

Jones-Ley, Susan, *Llamas, Woolly, Winsome, and Wonderful*. Photography by Susan, P.O. Box 1038, Dublin, Ohio 43017. $19.95 postpaid. 68 pages. Text with photos of llamas from across the country by the best known llama photographer.

Lewis, Beth, *A Handbook For Llamas: First Aid Techniques*. Second Edition, 1989. 2780 Merline Galice Road, Grants Pass, Oregon 97526. 76 pages. $10.00 postpaid. Short manual on First aid.

The preceding list was compiled by the International Llama Association and Rosana Hart.

Periodicals

The Backcountry Llama, Noel McRae, Editor, 2857 Rose Valley Loop, Kelso, Washington 98626. Newsletter about packing with llamas, published six times per year, $8.00/year.

Canadian Llama News, Margaret Brewster and Marie Lammle, Editors, 6012 Third St. SW, Calgary, Alberta, Canada T2H 0H9. Bi-monthly publication includes interest to llama owners in the U.S. as well as in Canada. $20.00/year.

Lana News, Virginia Christensen, Editor, P.O. Box 1882, Minden, Nevada 89423. Newsletter of the Llama Association of North America, published quarterly.

Llama Banner, P.O. Box 1968, Manhattan, Kansas 66502. Bi-monthly magazine with features, news and results of shows and events. $24.00/year.

Llama Life, Terry Price, Editor, 2259 CR 220, Durango, Colorado 81301. News and feature articles, ads, photos and excellent information for old and new breeders. Published quarterly, $16.00/year.

Llama Link, Jan and Dar Wassink, Editors, Drawer 1995, Kalispell, Montana 59903. Free monthly classified.

Llamas Magazine, Cheryl Dal Porto, Editor, 46 Main St., Jackson, California 95642. A must for every llama owner. Published eight times per year. Chocked full of information. $25.00/year.

Videotapes

All About Alpacas. A Gary Sanders/Eric Hoffman production. Gary Sanders, 1 Tunitas Creek Rd., Half Moon Bay, California 94019. Approximately thirty minutes. $49.95.

Breeding, Birthing and Newborn Care. Tape two of the series, *All About Llamas* with Paul and Sally Taylor. Taylor/Gavin Communications, Box 4323, Bozeman, Montana 59772. $41.95 postpaid. A sixty-minute practical video guide with handbook.

Five Star Llama Packing. Juniper Ridge Press, P.O. Box 338, Ashland, Oregon 97520. $41.95 postpaid. This two-hour tape shows experienced packers demonstrate all phases of llama packing.

Let's Go Packing. Tape #3 of the series, *All About Llamas.* Taylor/Gavin Communications, Box 4323, Bozeman, Montana 59772. $41.95 postpaid. Fifty minutes of basic training, llama care and packing.

Llama Basics, Tape #1 of the series, *All About Llamas*. Tyalor/Gavin Communicaitons, Box 4323, Bozeman, Montana 59772. $41.95 postpaid. Forty minutes. This is a basic introduction to llamas, including nutrition, housing, evolution and behavior.

Llama Reproduction: A Neonatal Clinic With LaRue Johnson, DVM, PHD. Juniper Ridge Press, P.O. Box 338, Ashland, Oregon 97520. 1989. $97.00 postpaid. Set of two tapes covers an actual clinic with hands on demonstrations. Topics are reproduciton and birth sequences.

Llama Training With Bobra Goldsmith: What Every Llama Should Know. Juniper Ridge Press, see address above. Two hours. $67.00 postpaid. Excellent guide to llama training.

T.E.A.M. With Llamas: A Trauma-Free Training Clinic with Linda Tellington Jones. Juniper Ridge Press, see address above. Set of two tapes, three and one half hours, $67.00 postpaid.

Training Llamas To Drive, with Bobra Goldsmith, Juniper Ridge Press, see address above. Two hours, $67.00 postpaid. This is an excellent tape for anyone who wants to train their llama to pull a cart.

Why Llamas? Juniper Ridge Press, see address above. Fifty minute tape. $31.95 postpaid. Interviews with llama owners and llamas doing everything from giving birth to taking part in obstacle races.

Note* Videotape information courtesy of Rosana Hart, Juniper Ridge Press.

Llama Equipment and Suppliers

BOOKS AND VIDEOTAPES

Barkman Animal Enterprises, 34190 Lodge Rd., Tollhouse, CA 93667
(209) 855-6227

Hartworks, Inc., P. O. Box 1278, Olympia, WA 98507 (800) 869-7342

Llamas Magazine Store, 46 Main St., Jackson, CA 95642 (209) 223-0466

Neon Llama Gift and Supply, 13417 Bowman Rd., Auburn, CA 95603
(800) 230-5262; email: neonllama@westsierra.com

EQUIPMENT

Neon Llama Gift and Supply, 13417 Bowman Rd., Auburn, CA 95603
Full line equipment, medical supplies, packs, gifts, etc. Free Catalog.
(800) 230-5262 Fax (530) 888-0298; email: neonlama@westsierra.com

JEWELRY AND COLLECTIBLES

NOSE-N-TOES, 4790 Luneman Rd., Placerville, CA 95667. A unique collection of llama inspired jewelry, Bolivian crafts, wearable art, and Andean CDs and cassettes. Free catalog. (800) 530-6391
Fax (530) 642-2378; email: wec3@ns.net

SPINNING EQUIPMENT

Switzer Land Alpacas and Llamas, Box 3800, Estes Park, CO 80517
(303) 586-4624

Services

Backpacking Adventures. Hurricane Creek Llamas, 63366 Pine Tree Rd., Enterprise, OR 97828-9705   (541) 432-4455.

Boarding. Llasa Llama Ranch, 11554 Rough & Ready Rd., Rough & Ready, CA 95975   (530) 432-8137.

Boarding. Barkman's Animal Enterprises, 34190 Lodge Rd., Tollhouse, CA 93667   (209) 855-6227.

Cria Care Consultation. Sandi Wilson, Llasa Llama Ranch, 11554 Rough & Ready Rd., Rough & Ready, CA 95975   (530) 432-8137.

Identification. Destron Microchips, Riley Identification Systems, 10800 Towne Rd., Carmel, IN 46032   (800) 552-6216.

Insurance. Aries Livestock Insurance Agency, Drawer A, Rich Hill, MO 64779   (800) 641-2072.

Insurance. Wilkins Livestock Insurance, Box 24, RR 1, Geneva, NE 68361   (800) 826-9441.

Pack Training. Northwest Passage Llamas,   (530) 432-3059. Email DMcneil863@aol.com

Photography. Photography by Susan, P.O. Box 1038, Dublin, OH 43017   (614) 889-0629.

Transportation. Jim Otte, Bozeman, MT   (406) 686-4666.

Transportation. Bill Egbert, Enumclaw, WA   (800) 426-0862.

Bibliography

Books

American Llama Show Association Handbook, 1990, Ocate, New Mexico.

Barkman, Paul and Betty. *A Well Trained Llama: A Trainer's Guide*. Tollhouse, California. n.p. 1985.

Creekmore, Hubert. *Daffodils Are Dangerous*. New York, New York: Walker & Company, 1966,

Dal Porto, Cheryl and Francie Greth-Peto, Eds. *Best of 3L Llama: The First Five Years*. N.p. 1985.

Ebel, Stan. "The Llama Industry in the United States". *The Veterinary Clinics of North America: Food Animal Practice*. Volume 5/number 1, March 1989, Johnson, LaRue. Ed. W.B. Saunders & Co. Philadelphia, Pa.

Escobar, Rigoberto Calle. *Animal Breeding and Production of American Camelids*. Lima, Peru: Talleres Graficos de ABRIl. 1984.

Faiks, Jim; Topzier, Phyllis; and Lyon, Jan Faiks. *Llama Training: Who's in Charge?* Big Lake, Alaska: N.p. n.d.

Fowler, Murray E. *Medicine and Surgery of South American Camelids*. Ames, Iowa: Iowa State University Presss, 1989.

_____,*Llama Medicine: Workshop Proceedings*. Santa Cruz, California, June 23-24, 1984.

Hart, Rosana. *Living With Llamas*. Ashland, Oregon: Juniper Ridge Press, 1985.

Haynes, N. Bruce. *Keeping Livestock Healthy*. Pownal, Vermont: Garden Way Publications, 1985.

Hoffman, Clare and Ingrid Asmus. *Caring for Llamas, A Health and Management Guide*. Livermore, Colorado: Rocky Mountain Llama Association, 1989.

Lewis, Elizabeth A. *A Handbook for Llamas: First Aid Techniques*. Bandon, Oregon: Stormy Mountain Press, 1986.

Siegmund, Otto H., Ed. *The Merck Veterinary Manual*. Rahway, New Jersey: Merck & Co., Inc. 1979.

Videotapes

Johnson, LaRue. "Llama Reproduction: A Neonatal Clinic." Part I, Ashland, Oregon: Juniper Ridge Press, N.d.

_____. "Llama Reproduciton: A Neonatal Clinic." Part II, Ashland, Oregon: Juniper Ridge Press, N.d.

Taylor, Paul and Sally. "Breeding, Birth and Newborn Care." Bozeman, Montana: Taylor/Gavin Communictions, N.c.

Articles

Abbott, Averill. "Show Tips." *Llama Life* 5 (Spring 1988): 16.

Barkman, Betty and Paul. "The Obstacle Course: An Excellent Means for Training the Llama and the Handler." *Llamas*, May/June 1986, 37-41.

Biggs, Stephen. "Backcountry Nutritional Needs of Llamas." *Llama Life* 6 (Summer 1988): 15.

_____, "Wilderness First Aid." *Llama Life* 5 (Spring 1988): 19.

Blanco, Marcia. "Form and Function." *Llama Life* 12 (Winter 1989-90): 10-11.

Bravo, P. Walter. "Breeding Practices in South America." *Llama Life* 9 (Spring 1989): 12.

_____, "Clues to Verify Copulation in Alpacas and Llamas." *Llama Life* 9 (Spring 1989):12.

Chlarson, Nancy A. "Hay Quality and Selection." *Llamas* March/April 1986, 58-59.

Fowler, Murray E. "Congenital/Hereditary Conditions in Male Llamas." *Llamas*, May/June 1988.

_____, "Foot and Mouth Disease." *Llamas*, January/February 1988, 89-92.

_____, "Form, Function, Conformation and Soundness," *Llamas*, November/December 1986, 45-53.

_____, "Rickets." *Llamas*, March/April 1990, 92-95.

_____, "Selenium, Friend or Foe." *Llamas*. March/April 1986, 37-43.

_____, "Skin Problems in Llamas and Alpacas," *Llamas*. July/August 1989.

Fowler, Murray E.; Joanne Paul; and Bravo, P. Walter. "Reproductive Hormones in Female Llamas and Alpacas." *Llamas*, September/October 1988, 35-37.

Frost, Bob and Michelle Brakebill. "Blood Typing to Verify Pedigrees." *Llama Life* 7 (Autumn 1988): 25.

Gatewood, Donna M. "General Health Considerations and Routine Maintenance of Llamas." *Llama Banner*, December/January 1990, 47-48.

Gibson, Coral. "Foot and Mouth Disease Strikes Canada: 1952 Epidemic Cost $130 Million." *Llama Life* 12 (Winter 1989-90): 8, 34.

Graham, Dale. "Breeding for the Best." *Llamas*, May/June 1988, 97-105.

_____, "Inbreeding, The Good, the Bad & the Ugly." *Llama Life* 7 (Autumn 1988): 22-23.

_____, "Why Register." *Llama Life* 9 (Spring 1989): 13, 30.

Greth, Francie. "Awaiting the Newborn." *Llamas*, September/October 1985, 61-63.

Hoffman, Eric. "The Alpaca Factor." *Llamas*, July/August 1986, 41-46.

_____. "The Blue Eyed Burden." *Llamas*, November/December 1986, 55-56.

_____. "Ethics & Genetics." *Llama Life* 5 (Spring 1988): 11, 21.

_____. "Hearst Herd Smaller Influence on Gene Pool Believed." *Llama Life* 5 (Spring 1988): 13.

Hook, Jim. "Caution, Llamas on Board." *Llamas*, January/February 1988, 29-35.

Hume, Charles. "Reproductive Methodology and Pregnancy Confirmation in the Llama," *Llamas*, September/October 1988, 38-43.

Hyder, Lynn. "Llama Shows: Prepare to Have Fun." *Llamas* May/June 1987, 89-91.

_____. "On Showing." *Llamas*, September/October 1987, 64-68.

Hyder, Judie. "Some Secrets to my Showmanship Success." *Llama Banner*, September/October 1988, 43-44.

Johnson, La Rue. "The Cold Weather Diet." *Llama Life* 8 (Winter 1988): 7.

_____. "EPA: A Troubling Parasite." *Llama Life* 12 (Winter 1989-90): 19.

Kaufman, H.D. "Is Your Watering Trough Heater Safe?" *Llama Life* 12 (Winter 1989-90): 33.

Koenig, Julie L. Farver. "Modes of Inheritance in the Llama and Wool Color Genetics." *Llamas*, September/October 1989, 49-56.

_____. "Production of the Genetically Superior Llama: Breeding Stock Selection, Mating Systems and Genetic Defects." *Llamas*, Stars of Tomorrow, Special Edition, Vol. 3 No. 7, 1989.

Leach III, James B. "Intubation of the Baby Llama." *Llamas*, May/June 1988.

Mayerle, Joan. "How to Control Flies Without Dangerous Chemicals." *Llamas*, May/June 1989.

McGee, Marty. "Selective Breeding: A Case for Moderation." *Llamas*, January/February 1989, 86-94.

Miller, Gary A. "Internal Parasites." *Llamas*, Herd Sire Edition 1989, 97-102.

Olsen, Richard. "Hybridization and Inbreeding: Roads to Ruin, Part I." *Llama Life* 7 (Autumn 1988): 6-7, 29.

_____. "Hybridization and Inbreeding: Roads to Ruin, Part II." *Llama Life* 8 (Winter 1988): 16-19, 20.

_____. "Roads to Ruin: Part III: Voodoo Economics." *Llama Life* 12 (Winter 1989-90: 6-7.

Patterson, Kay. "The Chief Sitting Bull/Zorro Story." Letters to the Editor, *Llamas*, September 1990, 10-12.

Rais, Jay. "Fencing." *Llamas*, July/August 1988, 25-31.

Robertson-Boudreaux, Jane. "Pasture Breeding? Controlled Breeding?" *Llamas*, Herd Sire Edition 1989.

Rolfing, Sue and Sheron Herriges. "Berserk Male Syndrome." *Llamas*, September/October 1987, 70-73.

Schoenthal, Daniel Weston. "The Question of Breeds." *Llama Life* 3 (Autumn 1987): 5.

_____. "Shearing." *Llama Life* 5 (Spring 1988): 5.

Sharp, Jamie. "The Hand Raised Llama," *Llamas*, November/December 1988.

_____. "Premature Llama Care." *Llamas*, May/June 1988, 81-84.

Smith, Brad. "Colostrum: Immunoglobulin Absorption in the Llama." *Llamas*, January/February 1990, 29-33.

_____. "Pregnancy Diagnosis in the Llama." *Llamas*, November/December 1988, 25-30.

Smith, Brad and Pat Long. "Pre-Purchase Exams in the Llama." *Llamas*, March/April 1989, 35-37.

Smith, Bradford B. and Patrick Long. "Preventative Health Care." *Llamas*, March/April 1988, 19-23.

Smith, Roland. "Berserk Male Syndrome: Effects of Inappropriate Imprinting." *Llama Life* 3 (Autumn 1987): 3, 8.

Sprouse, Brad. "Battle with the Meningeal Worm" *Llamas*, March/April 1986, 61-65.

Stevens, Judy. "Grooming tips." *Llamas*, September/October 1988.

Taylor, Paul. "The Berserk Male." *Llama Life* 9 (Spring 1989): 8.

"The Ten Most Prolific Studs." *Llama Life* 11 (Autumn 1989): 8.

Weston, Daniel. [Schoenthal] "Toenail Trimming." *Llama Life* 11 (Autumn 1989): 8.

Wielenga, Riny. "With Age in Mind." *Llamas*, May/June 1987, 19-23.

INDEX

About the Author

Sandi Burt Wilson owns and operates the Llasa Llama Ranch in historic Rough and Ready, California. She became interested in llamas in 1984 and has since bred eighteen champions. She is an active member of CAL-ILA, LANA, and ALSA, and was certified as a llama judge by the Alpaca and Llama Show Association in 1996.

In addition to raising llamas, Sandi is a real estate broker, writer, and pilot. She recently resumed her maiden name and is known in the llama community as Sandi Wilson.